THE PEOPLE'S NEWS

The People's News

Media, Politics, and the Demands of Capitalism

Joseph E. Uscinski

NEW YORK UNIVERSITY PRESS

New York and London

NEW YORK UNIVERSITY PRESS
New York and London
www.nyupress.org

© 2014 by New York University

References to Internet websites (URLs) were accurate at the time of writing.
Neither the author nor New York University Press is responsible for URLs that
may have expired or changed since the manuscript was prepared.

For Library of Congress Cataloguing-in-Publication data,
please contact the Library of Congress

ISBN: 978-0-8147-6033-8 (cl)
ISBN: 978-0-8147-6488-6 (pbk)

New York University Press books are printed on acid-free paper,
and their binding materials are chosen for strength and durability.
We strive to use environmentally responsible suppliers and materials
to the greatest extent possible in publishing our books.

Manufactured in the United States of America
10 9 8 7 6 5 4 3 2 1

Also available as an ebook

CONTENTS

ACKNOWLEDGMENTS

This work is the culmination of long hours of data collection, analysis, writing, and rewriting. The process has been greatly enjoyable and fulfilling. I always wanted to study news content, but after working on my own, I didn't feel I was quite "hitting it." Sitting down with one of my advisors, Brad Jones, we started from scratch and began to craft what would eventually become this book. I first have to thank Brad for helping to set me on this course.

The data collection efforts took about seven years. There are many people for me to thank for this, and I apologize for any errors of omission. First and foremost is Ryan Fitzharris—he is as familiar with this data as I am, and worked with me from the very beginning through the end. I am appreciative of both his hard work and his long-standing friendship. More recently, Alex Alduncin and Marlon Baquedano did an enormous amount of heavy lifting—both in terms of data analysis and in terms of reading through hundreds of hours of transcripts.

I need to thank my other advisors, Jan Leighley and Chad Westerland. Chad, in particular, worked with me rather closely in my final year at Arizona. My colleagues at the University of Miami, during the sometimes grueling sessions of our colloquium series, provided very thoughtful feedback—Greg Koger, Casey Klofstad, Joe Parent, Louise Davidson-Schmich, Merike Blofield, Fred Frohock, George Gonzalez, Chris Mann, Jon West, and Matthew Atkinson. Scholarship is more fun and productive with others, and I am grateful for the time and effort they invested in this work.

I am also grateful to Ilene Kalish and her staff. Ilene has been on board with this book since we first met in August 2010, and has been a great help in moving the book forward. I am greatly appreciative of the opportunity to publish with New York University Press.

I would of course be remiss if I did not thank those in my personal life who have helped and supported me so much during the last few years—for their love and support, Leilany, Benny, and Ruby; and my family, Mom, Dad, Kevin, Tracy, Amy, Gram, and Jack. My first introduction to the profession was back in 1993, in Dr. Egbert's American Government course at Plymouth State College. I took six more courses with him during my undergraduate career—he shaped my desire to be a political scientist and I am eternally grateful for that.

My main argument is that audience demands drive news firms to report the stories they report—news firms want to attract as large an audience as possible. This seems an intuitive argument, but my reading of the literature is that such economic models, particularly when it comes to explaining news content, have often been given short shrift. While university presses are somewhat shielded from raw profit motives, I could not help but be influenced by my own argument as I completed the work. My goal, once the analyses were complete, was to write a book that would appeal to as broad an audience as possible. I was less interested in "selling copy" per se than in spreading my arguments to anyone who might care to listen.

My personal interest in writing this book was to bring attention to a subject that I care very deeply about. I watch a lot of news. I care both about the content of the information and the way people respond to it. While I do not want to paint the past with rosy hindsight, I think the news environment has gotten worse, and will only continue on a downward trend. I do not want to imply that news is all "bad," but I think that as a society we are beginning to see the effects of a segmented news environment. I fear that without a common content or common dialogue, our democracy will not develop much further than it has. I also worry that so much of the precious available news space is wasted on low-quality news and on non-news. But even with these critiques, I am eternally grateful for the freedoms that are protected in this country that allow the news to be what it is, and that allow me to write this book.

1

Introduction

Whose News?

Most television news programs are designed to satisfy the
perceived appetites of our audiences. That may be not only
acceptable but unavoidable in entertainment; in news, however, it is the journalists who should be telling their viewers
what is important, not the other way around.
—Ted Koppel, January 29, 2006

After leaving the daily grind of the ABC News Division, veteran anchor
Ted Koppel tried his hand as a columnist for the *New York Times.* Prior
to his retirement in late 2005, Koppel had spent decades in the news business; he covered numerous heads of state, natural disasters, major wars,
and momentous elections. Rather than focus on the substance of any of
these major stories in his first column, Koppel chose instead to discuss a
problem he felt could negatively affect election outcomes, public policy,
and democratic procedures. In short, Koppel discussed a problem he felt
could damage the very fabric of American democracy. This problem is
the amount of audience influence over American news programming.

Koppel contended that news firms no longer provide the most important and consequential stories to audiences, an approach sometimes
called "traditional journalism." Instead, outlets fill precious space with
news designed to appease the audience's demands. This leaves audiences

without the information necessary to properly function in a democracy. Instead, Koppel argued, news producers have been too willing to abdicate their independent judgment and, as a substitute, adjust news content in response to ratings, audience demographics, and public opinion polls. He claimed that news firms chase audiences and profits at the expense of the public good. In other words, news outlets provide the news people *want* to know, at the expense of the news people *need* to know.

Koppel is not alone in these concerns; in fact, many in the news industry agree with his chilling assessment. For example, veteran CBS anchor Dan Rather commented, in typical Dan Rather fashion, "If we [try] to figure out what it is the audience wants and then try to deliver it to them, we're lost souls on the ghost ship forever." These concerns should not be dismissed as mere complaints by jilted practitioners who desire more power to exercise their own judgment. Unbiased experts outside of the newsroom have gathered mountainous evidence lending support to Koppel's assessments.

For decades, scholars have lamented the effect of money on the news. In explaining citizens' unsophisticated political views and scant knowledge of politics, preeminent media scholar Robert Entman (1989a:17) points to economic markets as the source: "The problem begins in the economic market, where news organizations compete for the audiences and advertising revenues necessary to maintain profitability and stay in business. The nature of both demand and supply . . . diminishes the press's autonomy." Noted media economics scholar James Hamilton (2005:351) points to the structure of incentives and the way they influence newsroom decision making:

> Although journalists may not explicitly consider economics as they consider the day's events, the stories, reporters, firms, and media that ultimately survive in the marketplace depend on economic factors. The decisions of producers and editors are driven by supply and demand: Who cares about a particular piece of information? What is an audience willing to pay for the news, or what are advertisers willing to pay for the attention of readers, listeners, or viewers? How many consumers share particular interests in a topic?

This is not to say that journalists, editors, and producers make *every* news decision with money, profitability, and audience share in mind. But, many news decisions are made for purely economic reasons. And, in order for news content to be influenced by economic concerns, those economic considerations need never be consciously on the minds of newspeople. As media economist John McManus (1995:309) puts it, decisions to report certain stories are "rarely made by consciously thinking through the components of business and journalism standards. . . . Reporters and editors may *feel* free to report the news as they see fit. But their freedom may seem larger than it is." News routines and organizational norms are shaped by powerful economic incentives, but newspeople may never know it.

Whether the influence of economic incentives over news content is conscious or unconscious, McManus (1992:789–90) argues that it leads to poorer-quality news:

> Adding viewers who possess the characteristics that advertisers value increases the station's revenues. The result is an economic pressure to attract as many viewers as possible. . . . National advertisers are paying, not for news quality, but for audience "quality" and quantity. All else held equal, advertisers can be expected to support the program generating the largest audience likely to purchase the products offered. . . . If the premium newscast drew no more of the "right kind" of viewers than a run-of-the-mill newscast, the station would not earn as great a profit as it might have with a less expensive production. Further, if the premium newscast were like the journalistically acclaimed *MacNeil/Lehrer NewsHour*, it might attract a smaller audience than competitors. The loyalty of that small viewership and the esteem with which journalists held the station might be admirable, but not bankable. . . . In television, and only to a slightly lesser degree in newspapers, advertising's "subsidy" makes a definition of quality based on popularity more profitable than one based on less widely shared professional or craft standards.

While there is broad agreement that the structure of economic incentives frustrates good journalism, many questions still remain. How much do economic incentives affect news content? Where can we see evidence of economics impacting substantive news content? What impact does a profit-driven news media have on society, and how can we correct the problems it creates? Journalists, such as Koppel and Rather, express great disdain for market-driven news decisions, but it is not clear that their reporting has been any more resistant to the influence of economics than that of any other journalist. Economic influence may be so strong that most people probably cannot even imagine a news environment not designed around the appeasement of audience demands.

It is this problem, the influence news markets have on news content, that *The People's News: Media, Politics, and the Demands of Capitalism* is about. There is no doubt that systemic economic forces, such as the need to sell advertising space and manage expenditures, determine the actions of news firms. But, the idea that economics determines the actual content of news reporting is more controversial. Unfortunately, despite the fact that journalists and scholars have recited concerns about the influence of economics over news reporting for decades, scholars have only recently taken a widespread interest in empirically testing the impact of supply and demand on news content. This has led to three problems in our understandings of news media. First, the actual effect of economic markets on news content remains elusive due to a lack of testing and specification. Second, the forces that drive news reporting continue to be debated by scholars. Third, the impact news outlets exert over audiences may be overestimated in relation to the impact that audiences have over news reporting.

The People's News seeks to fill these gaps in our understanding by detailing just how much of an impact market demands have on the news Americans consume. *The People's News* not only identifies the specific market demands that affect substantive news content but also provides a detailed account of the extent to which some of these demands affect news coverage. Along the way, *The People's News* explores the political ramifications of a market-driven news environment and provides insight into a series of long-standing debates that have puzzled researchers. For example, what makes a story "newsworthy"? What are the sources of news? How much do the media affect the audience's political opinions and behaviors? *The People's News* attempts to enlighten these debates with empirical evidence that will not only illuminate the way media scholars think about the construction of day-to-day news content but also refocus the public debate about the United States' vastly segmented contemporary news environment.

The remainder of this chapter introduces the major debates and concepts that subsequent chapters address in more detail. I begin with a discussion of how economic markets affect news outlets. A robust understanding of the way economic forces shape news content is vitally important given the crucial role news is expected to play in democratic society. Why do economics influence news content? How do economic concerns manifest in day-to-day reporting? What is the extent of this influence?

I then introduce the impact news has on democratic society. How does the news contribute to citizen knowledge, encourage good citizenship, and drive public opinion and public policy? How can the news media positively affect society, and can we see evidence of these positive effects? Unfortunately, the compiled evidence will suggest that while the news can exhibit strong and positive impacts on democratic society, it falls drastically short in the United States.

This chapter then introduces the three major theoretical paradigms that scholars have proffered to explain news content. The first, *traditional journalism*, argues that journalists *should* encourage and nurture good citizenship, most prominently by providing the information citizens need to effectively participate in democratic governance. I argue that American news outlets should follow traditional journalistic standards; however, the evidence presented will suggest that they do not. The second major theoretical paradigm to explain news content, *supply-side*, argues that those supplying the news, in or above the newsroom, choose what news to report and how to report it with little deference given to the demands of audiences. The third paradigm explaining news content focuses on the influence of economics over news. *Demand-side* points of view argue the opposite of supply-side models—that audiences, or those who consume the news product, drive news content. Much like producers of other products, news firms must produce a product that meets consumer demands. If news firms do not, their product will lose audience size, revenue, and viability. In discussing demand-side models, I discuss three different types of demands that news outlets may seek to meet: those for entertainment, those for information, and those for gratification. In introducing these demands, I provide examples of how news outlets may alter substantive news content to meet those different demands. This discussion is followed by the plan of the book, which delineates how each remaining chapter will demonstrate the influence of market demands on news content. To begin, I now examine the economic system that news firms operate within and explain how understanding the incentives of that system is vastly important to understanding the American news media.

Markets and the Media

In the United States, firms operate within a capitalist economic system and therefore must provide products appealing to a sizable number of consumers in order to incur a profit. Firms that fail to incur profits go out of business. Given that they operate in the same incentive structure, news firms are no different from the farmer's market on the side of the road or the international conglomerate selling software products worldwide. Just like those other companies, news firms must produce a product that people will consume at a price maximizing profits. Media scholars do concede that the economics of news is slightly different than that of many other products: news firms often earn revenue not by charging the end news consumer but instead by selling other companies access to those consumers through advertising space (Picard 2002). As McManus (1992:788) asserts, "Most commodities are simpler. . . . [Y]ou fork over the money directly. For news production it is more complicated. Most of the cost of creating both newspapers and newscasts is paid by a third party, advertisers."

In order to attract revenue from the sale of advertising space, news firms must maintain sizable audiences. If news firms do not attract a sizable audience with their product, their employees will lose their jobs, the company will be reorganized, and it will eventually go "belly-up." Simply put, news firms must provide a product people want to consume. So, despite the differences in who provides the actual income, news firms are little different from the farmer's market selling cucumbers to passersby or the conglomerate selling computer operating systems to other large conglomerates—all must provide products that people will willingly choose to consume in the face of alternatives.

To name but a few examples, the New York Times saw revenues of $2.4 billion and the news division at CBS brought in $424 million in revenue in 2010.[1] Given the financial stakes involved for news producers, it is little surprise that economic forces have often been indicted as the cause of what many consider to be low-quality news content. Thus, economic theories of news have been prominent in scholarly discussions (McChesney 1997; McManus 1994; Lacy 1992; Entman and Wildman 1992; Hamilton 2005). Perhaps the most important empirical study examining the role of markets in news is Hamilton's *All the News That's Fit to Sell: How the Market Transforms Information into News* (2004). This work provides perhaps the most exhaustive account of the way market demands drive news production. But while some scholars have invested effort in looking at markets to explain the news, economic theories have not gained universal acceptance. Some continue to believe that economic concerns are kept out of the newsroom and beyond the concern of those choosing and crafting stories for dissemination (see discussion in Fengler and Russ-Mohl 2008).

To bolster economic arguments, scholars in recent years have employed vast amounts of empirical data as well as sophisticated methods of analysis to estimate the effects of audience demands on news content (Powers 2001; Althaus et al. 2009; Dunaway 2008; Arnold 2004; Hamilton 2004; Zaller 1998; McDonald and Lin 2004; Dunaway 2012). These studies have provided direct evidence showing that the content and quality of news are greatly affected by audience demands. To name but one example, in a cross-sectional examination of U.S. newspapers, Gentzkow and Shapiro (2010) found that consumers' partisan preferences drive newspaper demand, and that that demand accounts for 20 percent of the observed variation in newspaper reporting. In other terms, political preferences translate into news preferences, and news preferences translate into actual news content.

Despite the emergence of new systematic evidence, most popular discussion of news economics skips over the impact of economics on news content. Instead, much of the discussion about media economics, especially in the last three decades, has focused on attempts by firm management to adapt to newer modes of delivering content and collecting advertising revenue. For example, much has recently been made of news outlets downsizing payrolls and closing foreign bureaus (e.g. Enda 2011). The corporatization (and near-monopolization) of the media has been a topic of frequent discussion as well (e.g. Pérez-Peña 2008). These changes have been met with much dismay, particularly by journalists who have faced dwindling job opportunities in recent years. But, the downsizing and adaptation present only a symptom of the much larger economic forces affecting news content long prior to recent decades.

As the earlier quotations from media scholars Hamilton and McManus suggest, economic models of news content are very much *structural* arguments. Much like actors in Charles Darwin's theory of evolution, or Adam Smith's "invisible hand," actors in the media need not be consciously aware of their incentive structure. They are simply punished if they fail to follow it. News firms that fail to attract audiences get restructured or go out of business, and journalists who displease editors, owners, and advertisers get fired (McManus 1995:309). Consider the recent restructuring at *Newsweek*. After seventy-nine years, the once-lauded news magazine is ceasing its print operations following years of dwindling sales.

Furthermore, actors need not ever admit to following their incentive structures even if they are consciously aware of it. This is why journalists, editors, producers, and owners rarely suggest that their product is intended to draw in audiences. Such an admission would be akin to a member of Congress claiming to have taken a vote on legislation in order to get reelected, rather than to make good public policy. Just as individual members of Congress always claim to act in the best interest of the people (even though many studies suggest that legislators are insincere and self-interested), news firms claim to abide by traditional journalistic standards that preclude the influence of money on reporting. Because newspeople rarely admit in public that economic concerns affect their reporting, smoking-gun confessions directly linking economic motives and subsequent news content will be rare.

A great deal of research shows that journalists respond to audience demands when constructing substantive news content. Polls of network television news correspondents indicate that almost a third feel directly pressured to report certain stories over others due to owners' or advertisers' financial concerns (Price 2003). And beyond direct pressure, competition for scarce jobs naturally leads journalists to favor profitability over "journalistic value." For example, journalists at online news outlets are judged by the number of clicks their articles receive. This sets up very clear incentive structures for journalists.

Given the incentives, there is little surprise that surveys have long shown that, as opposed to stories addressing pressing policy concerns, journalists define "news" as stories that "attract and hold the audience's interest" (Atkin and Gaudino 1984; Burgoon et al. 1982). Surveys also show that journalists value market demand in constructing news content: for example, half of journalists believe that public opinion polls are important to judging newsworthiness (Weaver 2005). It is safe to conclude that economic concerns bleed into journalists' news judgments.

In addition to journalists' incentives and inclinations to follow audience demands in reporting the news, it is important to note that news outlets are well suited to follow those demands as well. Not only do journalists believe it is important to meet audience demands, but they also have the necessary information to do so. Firms employ vast amounts of market research to determine what content best appeals to what audiences (McChesney 1997:23). Firms obtain sophisticated data detailing the demographics, opinions, and behaviors of their audiences, and they closely follow their market share (Ferguson 2004). Firms know who is watching, listening, reading, and clicking—they can make informed plans for catering to audiences based on hard data.

In addition to the availability of hard data, journalists, producers, and editors have first-hand knowledge of their audiences' likes, wants, and desires. Journalists are public figures—they are out and about, and they interact regularly with the audiences that they seek to satisfy. Journalists tend to have large Rolodexes, and talk to people at all levels of their communities. In short, newspeople are imbedded in audiences they seek to satisfy. Even before sophisticated methods of measurement became available, news firms had the ability to estimate audiences' demands.

Compiled studies indicate that, much like other businesses operating in capitalist systems, news outlets have the motive and means to temper their product to appeal to as wide an audience as possible. For most businesses, this would be great, and many may be tempted to view this as such. For example, a portion of Adam Smith's (1904) argument in favor of free markets states that when actors are allowed to act in their self-interest and freely follow the forces of supply and demand, they will achieve not only their private good but also a good for society. This is the case because firms would compete to provide the most desired product, and therefore consumers would be more likely to get the product they most want. In this logic, news that meets market demands should best serve the public. This is often referred to as the "invisible hand."

Unlike other businesses, however, news firms are granted unique constitutional protections that other types of businesses are not granted (Sanford and Kirtley 2005). News firms face relatively few rules or restrictions in constructing the news. Consider, for instance, the medical industry, which must conform to stringent government regulations. Not anyone can work as a doctor; doctors must get an approved education and receive the proper licensure and certifications. Medicines must be tested and approved by the Food and Drug Administration before they can reach the market. Patients cannot purchase any medicines they choose; medicines can only be prescribed by government-licensed medical professionals under government guidelines. The American government can regulate almost anything it wants.

In contrast, anyone can be a journalist, properly educated or not. No licensure, certification, or particular education is required. News is not tested, inspected, or certified by any government agency before firms provide it directly to the public. And, consumers can consume any news they want, any way they choose. Not only does the government not enact the same standards on news as on other products, but the Constitution specifically bars the government from doing so (Martin 2001).[2]

Why is the news so privileged in comparison to other industries? There are two main reasons. First, the constitutional framers viewed freedom of speech and of the press as a fundamental right, and did not want an overbearing government to curtail those rights. Second, the framers knew that a free and independent press is absolutely necessary in a participatory democracy. In exchange for constitutional protections, news firms therefore have a unique set of responsibilities in democratic society that other producers do not. These responsibilities include providing the information necessary to promote enlightened citizenship (Entman 1989a; Graber 1986).

Democracy therefore requires news outlets to exercise independent judgment when picking and choosing which information deserves mention and which does not (Entman 2005). This first requires that citizens have available news sources independent from the government so that politicians and officials can be both held accountable and kept limited in their power. But second, this also requires that citizens have available news sources free from their own demands. This is so that citizens are exposed to the news they *need* to know, whether they *want* to know it or not.

While laudable, keeping consumer demands out of news puts the demands of democratic society in direct conflict with the demands of capitalist society. Media economist Robert Picard (2005:338) refers to this as "a paradox, because it is recognized that commercially funded media require financial resources and strength to sustain and nurture their activities, but they cannot fully pursue their economic self-interests without harming optimal public service." News firms are therefore left potentially having to choose between providing two types of coverage: coverage that brings in audiences and revenue but contributes little to enlightened citizenship, and coverage that serves the greater public good but does not draw in audiences large enough to ensure profitability or even viability.[3] The requirements of democracy may be losing this conflict to the demands placed on news firms by capitalism.

The paradox news firms face between acting in their economic self-interest and acting for the public good provides a backdrop of market failure. A market failure occurs when the free market operates inefficiently or does not produce the optimal societal outcome. Many argue that the American news media fail to achieve optimal outcomes because the news media do not provide the information necessary for citizens to practice sophisticated citizenship and accordingly do a disservice to democratic society. By leaving citizens uninformed and starving on a low-information diet, the coverage that currently substitutes for high-quality news may dissuade citizens from participating, or may lead them to participate in ways counter to their interests. In this sense, the market failure is that audiences receive low-quality information and then act on it.

Despite the evidence of economic incentives invading news decisions, low-quality news dominating the news space, and citizens generally being uninformed, it has been nonetheless difficult to get broad agreement on the argument that markets drive news coverage and quality. Those on the ideological economic Right, because they do not want to admit that what best serves the market does not best serve society, argue that a market failure is not occurring in the news media since the public gets exactly what it wishes. Media scholar Robert Entman (1989a:17) elucidates this logic:

> Because most members of the public know and care relatively little about government, they neither seek nor understand high-quality political reporting and analysis. With limited demand for first-rate journalism, most news organizations cannot afford to supply it, and because they do not supply it, most Americans have no practical source of the information necessary to become politically sophisticated.

In short, if people demand low-quality news, that is exactly what they will receive under current arrangements—whether it serves the demands of democracy or not. As a consequence, this initial market failure may lead to a second form of market failure: negative externalities on third parties. In democracies, we all have to live with decisions made by majorities of our fellow citizens. If people only have access to low-quality or, even worse, incorrect information, then the decisions those people subsequently make for all of society will probably be as poor as their information environment. Everyone suffers.

A story about market failure could be written about many industries, and whether or not one buys the idea that poor news quality can be categorized as a market failure, the difference here is that the failures of the American news media carry intrinsic political implications. Low-quality news provides a low-quality information environment for democratic decision making. Therefore, the impact of markets on news content is as much a story of political failure as it is of economic failure.

Citizens must self-rule in democratic societies. They must choose between different leaders and opposing policy alternatives. The news media should impact citizens' opinions and behaviors by providing the necessary information to make choices in their best interest. But, as Koppel warned in his inaugural column, when outlets construct content that sacrifices the interests of the public to serve their own economic interests, they leave citizens without the information necessary to make knowledgeable decisions. Thus, the economic forces affecting the news media can have far-reaching political consequences for the whole of society. I now demonstrate how news media can impact citizens' knowledge, participation, and opinions, as well as public policy. The following discussion will show that the news media sacrifice their full potential to positively impact society in exchange for meeting market demands.

News Impact

Researchers have spent nearly a century investigating the impact of news media on mass political opinion and behavior as well as on public officials and policy. Do the news media shape audience opinions? Can the news affect political behaviors, such as the choices to vote and whom to vote for? What effects does the news have on election outcomes and subsequent public policy? These lines of inquiry, usually referred to as *media effects research*, have contributed greatly to our understanding of the media.

In chapter 2, I will discuss in greater detail the development of media effects research, but for now, readers should note that while there continues to be rigorous debate about the power of the media to affect attitudes, behavior, and policy, many credible studies indicate the impact of news to be immense and far-reaching. Therefore, understanding the origins of the actual content that potentially influences people and policy is very important. In this section, I briefly discuss how news affects citizens' knowledge, democratic citizenship, and public policy. In doing this, I will explain how economic incentives mediate the potentially large positive effects that news outlets could have on democratic governance.

Learning

Given that democracy calls upon citizens to make far-ranging decisions that potentially affect everyone, an electorate with a robust understanding of current political, economic, and societal conditions is highly desirable. Some argue that citizens *must* have a requisite amount of knowledge to make informed and rational decisions—the alternative is likely to be poor decision making (e.g. Caplan 2008). Imagine living in a country where millions of ignorant and uninformed people were going to make choices that directly impacted your life. Such an arrangement would probably leave you feeling as though you were in a rather precarious situation.

On the other hand, others argue that the public, ignorant of current affairs or not, thinks and acts rationally in the aggregate (Page and Shapiro 1992). This argument assumes that ignorance is randomly distributed in varying directions, so that the ignorant and uninformed masses will cancel each other out in the aggregate. It is left to a small group of informed citizens to make the "right" choices for everyone. This does not necessarily sound like a bad arrangement, except that unfortunately, this is not the case: errors in thought, often stemming from a lack of authoritative information, are often biased in one direction or another. This bias in the masses is often far too large for a small group of informed citizens to overcome (Caplan 2008), and thus the electorate may make public policy decisions out of ignorance (Althaus 2003). Democratic society therefore requires an informed electorate to make sound policy decisions.

How can we know if citizens "know enough" to effectively participate in democratic governance? According to media scholar Thomas Patterson, one test of an informed citizen is to measure "the amount of current-affairs information in that citizen's head" (2005:191). Given the necessity of providing information, the job of providing that information (by default) falls to the media. As Patterson argues, "No other source can routinely provide it" (2005:191). Given the expectation that the news media will provide relevant current-affairs information, two questions arise: (1) Can information in the news media impact citizen knowledge? and (2) How much information do outlets transmit?

To answer the first question, scholars have for years tested the effect of news exposure on citizens' factual political knowledge. In short, American citizens generally appear to be uninformed. When asked even basic surveillance questions about politics (Schudson 1998:70; Graber 1994), or questions about specific policies (Gilens 2001), they are unable to provide correct answers. Recall the popular "Jay-Walking" segment on *The Tonight Show with Jay Leno*: Leno's producers hit the street and ask people basic questions about American history and politics. Hilarity ensues because the interviewees can't answer even basic questions. Despite the laughter, the segment offers a sad commentary on the state of affairs. On the brighter side, scholars have repeatedly shown that exposure to news sources can increase citizen knowledge (Tan 1980; Tichenor et al. 1970; Conway et al. 1981; Barabas and Jerit 2009; Jerit et al. 2006; Weaver 1996; Eveland et al. 2005), and perhaps alleviate the ignorance highlighted by Leno.

In addition, different mediums of news (print, televised, internet) produce different levels and types of learning (Chaffee and Frank 1996;

Garramone and Atkin 1986; Wade and Schramm 1969; Vincent and Basil 1997; Baum 2003; Eveland et al. 2004). For example, Eveland, Marton, and Seo (2004) find that the readers of internet news stories do not learn as much factual information as consumers of other sources of news, but instead, they are able to gain denser and more interconnected knowledge structures due to the hyperlinked information in online news stories. Perhaps most importantly, recent studies show that information-rich news environments lead to more learning than information-poor news environments (Jerit et al. 2006; Prior 2005). For example, Barabas and Jerit (2009) show that the volume, breadth, and prominence of policy-specific news coverage increase the public's knowledge of the topics covered. In all, the evidence shows that the news media can induce learning, and when news provides higher-quality information, more learning occurs.

People *can* learn, and learning depends on the media environment. So, how much information do news outlets actually transmit? According to the compiled evidence, the answer to this question unfortunately appears less positive. For years, researchers have found that most news content generally lacks relevant policy-oriented information (Belt and Just 2008). Instead, popular outlets fill space with entertaining, but policy-devoid, information (Grabe et al. 2001). This type of information is sometimes referred to as "soft" or "human-interest" (Prior 2005). "Hard" traditional news programs may sacrifice meaningful news for softer stories, while newer news programming has been developed to report mostly "softer" stories. In either case, news firms provide poor-quality news in exchange for audience size. Although this style of reporting draws audiences in, this type of coverage generally lacks the information needed for consumers to practice informed citizenship (Rosenstiel et al. 2007).[4]

Even leading up to major elections (precisely when citizens have immediate need for relevant information), news outlets concentrate on daily poll results, candidate miscues, contrived scandals, and other information quite disconnected from policy relevance (Patterson 1994). During campaigns, this type of entertaining (though policy-devoid) coverage is referred to as "horse-race" or "game-schema" coverage. Think, for instance, of the difference between a story providing a candidate's standing in the latest daily tracking poll versus a story about that candidate's suitability for office. Because citizens appear to desire policy-devoid coverage (Baum 2003), audience demand is often cited as the cause of the low quality. For example, when given a choice, people tend to choose the nonsubstantive news over the more substantive (Iyengar et al. 2004).

The basic argument is that news firms attempt to cast as wide a net as possible with their product by "dumbing it down," or providing only the most provocative style of coverage; this strategy is seen by some as chasing the lowest common denominator (Entman 1989a:17). "Dumbed down" stories even take up precious news space on traditional news outlets like *NBC Nightly News*: "Fair to say it was only a matter of time before someone would think of hitting the TV 'paws' button in a whole new way. Yes, a cable channel for dogs is finally here!"
(Holt, NBC [6:30] p.m., April 28, 2012).

Audiences interested in receiving more sophisticated information continue to consume the low-quality news because they have few other places to go, or they may find *some* pertinent information after wading through the "softer" noninformative news (Giles 2003:218). But, many assume that the nonsubstantive coverage provided is the most important and highest-quality news possible, and never know to search for better. The desire to attract large audiences drives outlets to forgo valuable policy information. This, in turn, leaves the electorate too ignorant to effectively participate.

The news media can influence learning, and potentially improve democratic decision making. However, the news media do not reach their potential, and instead leave many starving on a low-information diet. To continue the discussion of how the news impacts society, the next section examines how the news media contribute to democratic citizenship.

Encouraging Democratic Citizenship

Besides transmitting relevant information, the news can also encourage quality citizenship. A quality citizen participates regularly, consumes relevant information for decision making, and actively supports the democratic system. News can play a powerful role in socializing citizens into the democratic system by transmitting norms of behavior, promoting positive attitudes toward the system, and encouraging participation.

Media socialization begins at or before adolescence. Studies show that exposure to news during childhood can pique political interest, increase social capital, and prime future political discussion and participation (Atkin and Gantz 1978; Garramone and Atkin 1986; Romer et al. 2009). As citizens enter into adulthood, media use can lead to "better understanding of the political world and may provide a stronger cognitive base for political participation" (Sotirovic and McLeod 2001:273). News usage may even facilitate forms of participation, including interpersonal discussion, speaking out, and voting (McLeod et al. 1999; Newton 1999).

News outlets generally do a good job of promoting participation and engagement by labeling upcoming elections as "important" and voter participation as "mattering." During the primary season of 2011–2012, the broadcast and cable news networks referenced elections as the "most important" 136 times. In the three months running up to presidential elections, they did this 297 times in 2008 and 203 times in 2004.[5] The media appear to label every upcoming national election as "the most important in our lifetime," and while this may or may not be true, this type of encouragement is good because it probably fuels engagement in the system and active participation. We would not want news that actively discouraged engagement and participation by ignoring, underplaying, or deeming irrelevant important political decisions.

Despite the positive impact that news coverage could (and should) have on quality citizenship, it still has yet to reach its potential. To name the most prominent facet of news inhibiting good citizenship, news content provides a predominantly negative view of society in general, and of politics more specifically (Patterson 1996). News outlets rarely highlight the "good"; instead, violence, scandal, criminal activity, and other negative stories dominate headlines (Grabe et al. 2001; Lichter and Noyes 1996; Sabato et al. 2000; Farnsworth and Lichter 2010). Researchers have long noted that negativity prevails in the news, even when reality paints a more positive picture. A study in the 1990s of both national and local news showed that in terms of both the number of stories and the amount of time devoted to them, more than half of the news depicted violence, conflict, and suffering; these stories were further emphasized by appearing earlier in the broadcasts (Johnson 1996). And, the language journalists use in reporting paints a negative picture of the world as well. In 2011, the cable and broadcast news networks used the words "shocking," "disturbing," and "frightening" in 944 news segments.[6] For example, political conflict, which in the United States usually involves little more than lukewarm civil disagreement between politicians, are often referenced by reporters as overtly violent acts when they are nothing of the sort. Let me demonstrate with but three examples from the nightly network news programs (italics added):

And it's not every day *the President of the United States launches a rocket at the Supreme Court.* But it happened today, setting the stage for a kind of *battle of the titans* over health care and that history making decision before the court right now. ABC's Jake Tapper gives us the *blow by blow.* (Sawyer, ABC [6:30] p.m., April 2, 2012)

[His rivals] are going to do everything they can over the next ten days to slow down [Romney's] momentum, *keeping him from steamrolling* his way to the nomination. *They're unleashing a series of brutal attacks* against him here in South Carolina where *presidential politics can be like a knife fight.* (Crawford, CBS [6:30] p.m., January 11, 2012)

While the rest of the nation watches, *Washington has blown up into a caustic partisan fight and a showdown is coming* over the power of the American president. . . . This contempt vote comes after the Obama White House, for the first time, invoked executive privilege. *Charges of stonewalling and cover-ups are flying,* the kind of stuff we first learned during the Watergate era. And for those not following the complexities of all of it, *it just looks like more of our broken politics and vicious fights now out in the open.* (Williams, NBC [6:30] p.m., June 20, 2012)

Not only do news outlets portray events in a negative light, but they often sacrifice the truth to do so. High-profile examples of firms reporting gloom and doom in the face of truth are legion (Heath 1996). For example, in the 1970s, even though the world's supply and quality of arable land, natural resources, food, and energy had been increasing for decades due to heightened efficiency, false bad news about population growth, natural resources, and the environment was published widely—and in the face of overwhelming amounts of contradictory evidence (Simon 1980).

To name but another example, in the 1990s it became conventional wisdom that parents spent 40 percent less time with their children than they had thirty years earlier. This statistic was cited more than fifty times by news organizations. Unfortunately, there was no evidence whatsoever to support any such decline in parent-child interaction (Whitman 1996).

Whether reporting false information or simply highlighting negativity, overtly negative news keeps the media from maximizing the positive effects it could have on sophisticated citizenship. Negative news can instill anxiety and sadness and create for some the impression that "the entire world is falling apart" (Lewis 1994:157; Johnston and Davey 1997). Scholars have argued that media negativity can create a "mean world effect" in which people overestimate crime rates, underestimate the benevolence of others, and as a consequence withdraw from social activities (Putnam 1995).

The mean world effect spills over into politics. The perverse view of reality created by negative coverage leads to feelings of inefficacy, cynicism, "malaise," and distrust (Cappella and Jamieson 1996; Valentino et al. 2001; Forgette and Morris 2006; Robinson 1976; Mutz and Reeves 2005; Patterson 1994; Bennett 1997). These feelings may then lead to skewed public priorities: for example, increased spending on criminal punishment and the increasing severity of criminal sentences are more correlated with crime coverage than with actual rates of crime (which have been historically decreasing) (Gilliam et al. 1996). The negative coverage may also result in muted political participation and substandard citizenship (Fallows 1997). People may choose to sit it out, rather than get involved in a chaotic and dangerous world.

What drives the overabundance of negative and cynical news coverage? Scholars often cite market demands: citizens simply prefer negative news. Studies of news going as far back as the 1940s show that citizens prefer negative headlines and, because of this, negative headlines sell better than positive ones (Allport and Milton 1943; Winship and Gordon 1943; Meffert et al. 2006). However, despite audiences' apparent desire for it, there exists a glaring irony: negativity is one of the leading complaints citizens continually make about the news (e.g. Haskins 1981).

This irony appears to be the product of evolutionary psychology: audiences may use the news as a way of surveying threats in the environment (Shoemaker 1996). Thus, when audiences view news that induces fear or anger, they pay closer attention (Newhagen 1998). This response may be unconscious, and audiences may not even know they are doing it. The logic is evolutionary: for example, if audiences see news about a rape in the parking lot, they know to avoid the parking lot (or to at least carry pepper spray). This unconscious desire to survey threats, perhaps to protect ourselves and our families, is not necessarily bad, but it does create a market demand. Problems arise because modern society has made it easier to appease this surveillance function with threats that are neither proximate nor probable, and news firms have been all too willing to capitalize upon such threats anyway. The real-world effect is that, because of the overly pronounced negative news coverage, audiences overestimate threats, and, as a result, withdraw from the social activities that lead to enlightened citizenship (Putnam 1995; Romer et al. 2003). By meeting these subconscious demands for negative information, news firms do democratic society a disservice by creating a negative externality (Hamilton 1998). Negative news may actually create a more negative world.

In examining the impact of news, I have so far discussed news influence over the amount of knowledge in citizens' heads, and the impact of news coverage on democratic citizenship. I now discuss the impact that news coverage has on mass political opinions and subsequent public policy.

Influencing Public Opinion and Policy

The effect of news coverage on political opinions and behaviors has been widely studied for nearly a century, and the variety of identified effects is wide-ranging. The study of media effects has faced, and continues to face, several impediments, the foremost being that it is difficult to link mass opinions and behaviors to singular causes such as the media. But with this said, it is widely acknowledged that the news media exert significant influence over citizens. Because the people rule in democracies, news outlets can therefore *indirectly* impact public policy and election outcomes. The news influences opinions, those opinions are translated into mass political behavior, and policy changes as a result. In addition, the news can also *directly* affect leaders and policy. The news can highlight certain topics, and leaders will subsequently address those topics with new policy initiatives. I now discuss two broad powers news outlets possess: (1) the ability to focus both citizens' and governmental agendas and (2) the ability to directly affect political opinions and behaviors.

Perhaps the most widely accepted effect of the news is its ability to set the issue agenda (or priorities) for both the public and the government (McCombs 2004). According to agenda-setting theory, the media report issues, and then the audience adjusts its ranking of issue salience to accord with the media's agenda. Put another way, the media have the ability to tell audiences what issues are important and in need of attention (and consequently, which are not). For example, if news outlets repeatedly highlighted stories about the economy, citizens would believe that the economy is highly important and in need of attention. If outlets stopped reporting about the economy, citizens would no longer believe it was quite so significant. By modifying the public's issue concerns, the media can consequently affect the way citizens evaluate leaders and candidates: studies show that citizens judge leaders according to the issues salient in the media (Iyengar et al. 1982). So, if outlets highlighted economic stories and citizens subsequently viewed the economy as highly important, citizens would begin to judge leaders on the basis of their economic performance. Through this process, termed "priming," the news media can impact evaluations of political leaders and potentially affect election outcomes. Chapter 2 will explore these effects more fully.

Beyond indirect influence over political outcomes, the news media can also directly impact the actions of leaders and institutions. Research shows that the news can set the issue priorities not only for government actors at all levels but in the private sector as well (Walgrave and Van Aelst 2006; Erfle et al. 1990). The news can drive congressional policy: studies show that news attention can alter congressional attitudes and, in turn, affect major policies, including spending policies (Cook and Skogan 1991; Trumbo 1995; Baumgartner et al. 1997a). News attention can also spur government attention to long-ignored social problems; for instance, news stories about the issue of child abuse brought about legislation from both Congress and several state legislatures (Nelson 1984). Even the presidency, a position designed for the exertion of independent leadership, follows, rather than leads, the news in many instances (Edwards and Wood 1999). For example, studies show that the State of the Union address, a speech supposedly used to push the president's agenda, often follows the issue agenda of previous news coverage (Wanta et al. 1989).

Beyond setting agendas, the news can also affect what citizens *think*. The news can directly affect citizens' opinions about leaders and foreign and domestic policy (Jordan and Page 1992; Bartels 1993; Entman 1989b). And, beyond simply affecting isolated attitudes, the news can lead to change in broad-based belief systems (Zaller 1991). The ability of the news media to affect attitudes can then impact election outcomes and public policy. For example, social scientist Tim Groseclose (2011) estimates that the news media have turned an America that would vote like a solid red state sans media intervention into an America that votes more "purple."

The tone of coverage during campaigns can lead to noticeable changes in attitudes towards candidates: positive coverage leads to higher favorability while more negative coverage leads to lower favorability (Druckman and Parkin 2004; Barker and Lawrence 2005; Joslyn and Ceccoli 1996). Beyond direct effects over candidate evaluations, the news can indirectly affect voter turnout and choice (Lott 2004; Della Vigna and Kaplan 2007; Gerber et al. 2006; Sheilds et al. 1995). For example, the media can affect the way citizens view objective conditions. During the presidential election campaign of 1992, the news portrayed the economy as much worse than any objective measure of economic performance would have suggested (Goidel and Langley 1995). The media's negative portrayal of the economy (independent of actual conditions) led citizens to evaluate the economy more negatively (Hetherington 1996). These negative evaluations, in turn, led Americans to vote against President George H. W. Bush on Election Day, and elect Bill Clinton instead.

To be clear, the exact effect of the news media over public opinions is hotly contested, and subsequent chapters will suggest that those effects, in some circumstances, have been overestimated. But given the evidence, journalists do have great power in society: the news can, in many ways, affect the course of history. As long-time journalism scholar Maxwell McCombs argues, this power creates "a situation that confronts journalists with a strong ethical responsibility" (2004:20). With this ethical responsibility, one would hope that the media would follow traditional journalistic standards. This involves (1) presenting information in a way that does not attempt to exert undue influence for the purpose of affecting political outcomes; and (2) using independent judgment to decide which information to report and how to report it rather than abdicating news decisions to other interests. (I will discuss traditional journalism in more detail in the following sections.)

Unfortunately, the available evidence suggests that news outlets have abdicated their independent judgment in favor of following audience demands. This has led to a perversion of the media's agenda-setting power so that news firms design content to draw in audiences, and this news, which is otherwise unimportant, becomes an issue priority for audiences. To provide but one example, in November 2011, the CBS show *60 Minutes* reported a story summarizing the recent book *Throw Them All Out* by Peter Schweizer. The story, like the book, argued that congresspeople enter Congress with modest wealth, but because of their access to information about the stock prospects of particular companies, leave rich. Public opinion polls at the time showed that Congress had historically low approval ratings of about 10 percent. As a result, a news story depicting Congress as a bunch of corrupt hucksters fit in well with contemporary public sentiment. Of course, the evidence of corruption, both in the book and in the news report, was based on little more than anecdote. The report went viral on the internet and received sustained coverage in most major news sources—after all, the public loves tales of scandal and skullduggery.

Responding to nothing other than the intense coverage (this had not been an issue prior to the *60 Minutes* story), on March 15 Congress passed federal legislation, the STOCK Act, which prohibited inside trading by congresspeople, and President Obama signed the bill into law April 4, 2012. The bill did little more than make illegal a practice that was already illegal. But even more ironically, at the time there was very little evidence to suggest that members of Congress had used insider knowledge, or had benefited from their positions in any way. In fact, the best evidence available suggested that congresspeople's portfolios underperform the market, and by significant margins (Eggers and Hainmuller 2011). But stopping the "corruption" became a congressional priority anyway, because *60 Minutes* had a financial incentive to pander to viewers with shoddy information.

Beyond chasing audience opinions, economists have long shown that by "slanting news," outlets can incur profits by appealing to one segment of the audience (Baron 2006; Mullainathen and Shleifer 2005). To name but one example, in a study of local newspapers, Pollock et al. (2006a) found that coverage of gay rights varied according to the political predispositions of the intended local audiences. Conservative populations received conservatively tilted news about gay rights while liberal audiences received liberally tilted news addressing gay rights. Despite the ethical responsibility that comes with the ability to influence the opinions and behaviors of citizens and leaders, outlets appear to abdicate their independence in exchange for what their audiences demand.

Having examined the impact of news, the discussion now turns to examine three major theoretical paradigms explaining news content. Where does news come from? What drives conceptions of newsworthiness? The following sections will suggest answers to these questions.

The Nature of News

Thus far, I have argued that the news can impact how well people fulfill their duties as citizens. The news can inform the masses, encourage trust in the democratic system, and shape citizens' political opinions and behaviors. The news can also affect the way leaders think and act on important policy questions. The news is powerful. But, in exchange for this unregulated power, media outlets have certain responsibilities. I have presented evidence thus far suggesting that economic incentives have led news outlets to shirk those responsibilities. The influence of economics has led news to negatively impact citizens' willingness and ability to competently participate in this country. Thus, this book is couched in concerns about the media's role in fostering and encouraging democratic governance.

In order to demonstrate more fully the negative impact of markets on news content, we must explore the vigorous debate about the nature of news. This debate centers on three general models explaining the sources of news content: traditional journalism, supply-side, and demand-side. Models of traditional journalism argue that news should come from independent journalistic judgment. Supply-side models argue that news content is determined by those supplying the news. Demand-side models argue that audience demand determines news content. I detail these three models below.

Traditional Journalism

There are many definitions of traditional democratic journalism; some of these stem from news outlets and from journalists' professional associations. Other definitions stem from scholars who have devoted many volumes to the topic. One professional organization, the Society of Professional Journalists, provides a list of "ethics" that focuses on reporting truth, minimizing harm to sources and subjects, acting independently, and being accountable (Journalists 1996). Political communication scholar Robert Entman (Entman 2005:54) provides five "Key Journalistic Standards": accuracy, balance, checks on pure profit-maximization, democratic accountability, and editorial separation.

Other scholars focus not on mechanical procedures but on the goals pursued by news organizations. Doris Graber (1986), for example, provides five functions of news media, taking a slightly different vantage point than Entman: reflecting diversity of opinion, informing citizens with needed information, communicating with government officials on behalf of citizens, expressing unpopular minority views, and detecting abuses of power. Regardless of how various scholars and organizations define "traditional journalism," these definitions typically distill down to three general facets: (1) providing necessary information, (2) encouraging democratic participation, and (3) setting agendas and shaping opinions. For purposes of space, I will keep the following discussion of these three aspects of traditional journalism brief.

First, journalists should provide the information necessary for consumers to practice advanced citizenship. In liberal democracies, citizens are asked to self-govern. This requires that citizens choose between opposing candidates and varying policies. News sources should lead citizens to understand competing alternatives. What are the candidates' espoused policies? How will these be implemented? What will be the short- and long-term effects? Without robust sources of current information, citizens would be making significant and far-reaching choices without the information necessary to make those choices (Entman 1989a:17; Graber 1986).

As part of providing the necessary information, journalists should also act as a "watchdog." As Graber (1986:258) puts it, the press should act as "the citizens' eyes and ears to detect and report corruption, abuses of power, and other misconduct by government officials." In this, the news encourages the powerful to act in the public interest by exposing (or threatening to expose) bad behavior to the public (Bennett and Serrin 2005). The press need not ever report corruption if none exists; simply the threat of exposure should be enough to encourage honest dealings.

Second, news should encourage democratic participation and transfer political norms. The news, by its very nature, should introduce transparency into the system (Francke 1995). This then should instill in the masses feelings of trust, inclusion, and efficacy. This may involve reaching out to marginalized groups, giving voice to all sides of the debate, and encouraging audiences to engage in the system (Graber 1986). Traditional journalism should also directly encourage participation, socialize audiences into democratic norms of behavior, and transfer political culture to viewers.

Third, news should set agendas and shape opinions. The news should bring to attention problems that need resolution, and explicate the potential solutions for those problems. This is a grave responsibility that requires that journalists provide information independently and in an unbiased manner. In pluralistic democracies, competing interests (interest groups, businesses, political parties, movements, etc.) attempt to shape public policy by influencing the media and public opinion in a way that favors their preferred outcome. An independent source of news would not act as a shill for any interest, but rather would critically evaluate the claims and proposed policies of all, without favor (e.g. Collins 2001). In addition, and just as important, journalists will not shape the news to favor the preexisting biases of their audiences. Journalists should provide the needed news, not the gratifying news. Thus, journalists should exercise their own judgment in choosing (1) the stories that warrant reporting and (2) how to report those stories. This would allow citizens to evaluate proposed policies with a robust supply of unbiased information.

Supply-Side Models

Supply-side (or top-down) models argue that, as in traditional journalistic models, news suppliers should decide the content of news independently. But unlike in traditional journalism, in the supply-side model, the welfare of democracy is of little concern. Supply-side models argue that forces above the audience, perhaps in the newsroom, perhaps above the newsroom, dictate news without much thought given to the audience's preferences or needs. Scholars have argued that a variety of supply-side actors exert control over the news; these include economic elites, government leaders, news firm owners, and journalists. I briefly describe the most popular of these arguments and then demonstrate the limits of the supply-side paradigm.

To begin, the Propaganda Model proposed by Edward Herman and Noam Chomsky (Herman and Chomsky 1988; Chomsky 1989) argues that capitalist elites, in a conspiratorial plot, control news content. In this model, news outlets portray the political and economic status quo in an overly positive light while criticizing alternative forms of government and economic distribution. This is done to keep capitalist elites in power by maintaining public support for the current economic system. A slight variation of this model, discussed by Ben Bagdikian (2004), similarly argues that media corporations in the United States act as a cartel with the intention of manufacturing in the populace right-wing values that favor the economic status quo.

A similar model proposed by George Gonzalez (Gonzalez 2005a, 2005b) is that owners of news outlets, in conjunction with other economic elites, will work to pursue economic development initiatives driven mainly by elites. News programs, therefore, following the wishes of their ownership and management, will attempt to gain favor for preferred policies.

Lance Bennett's indexing model presents a similar conception of top-down control, except in this case, the government, rather than economic elites, controls most news content (Bennett 2009). Bennett argues that (1) government sources dominate reporting to the exclusion of alternative voices and (2) news firms rely on "official" accounts of events from government officials to the exclusion of other accounts. Thus, the agenda of government officials, rather than journalists or advocacy groups, directs the flow of information, thereby limiting the range of alternatives presented to the public.

Another supply-side model involves the biases housed within news organizations. According to this model, journalists and/or news owners allow their ideological biases to color the reporting (Larcinese et al. 2007; Groseclose 2011). This may happen unwittingly or more purposively. Thus, the impact on reporting can be more subtle (e.g. Groseclose and Milyo 2005; Puglisi 2011) or more pronounced if it is intended as advocacy for a policy, candidate, or party (e.g. Goldberg 2009). For example, in a study of local newspapers, Puglisi and Snyder (2008) find that Democratic-leaning newspapers give more coverage to scandals involving Republican politicians than scandals involving Democratic politicians, while Republican-leaning newspapers do the opposite. But, whether one believes that newspeople transmit a liberal or conservative bias, the argument assumes that these preferences are transmitted without much concern for the tastes of the audience.

In recent decades, studies have shown that newspeople vote overwhelmingly Democratic and tend to support liberal causes by wide margins (Lichter et al. 1986). For example, a survey of journalists in 2005 showed that they voted for Democrat John Kerry over Republican George W. Bush two to one, they identify as Democrat over Republican three to one, and they identify as liberal over conservative three to one.[7] In contrast, the public voted for Bush over Kerry, and identifies as Republican and conservative roughly equally to Democratic and liberal. Given this, most popular arguments suggest a liberal bias on the part of most of the mainstream media (e.g. Goldberg 2002). As long-time journalist and media critic Bernard Goldberg (2009:4) argued about the 2008 election,

> Sure, mainstream journalists always root for the Democrat. But this time it was different. This time journalists were not satisfied merely being partisan witnesses to history. This time they wanted to be real players and help determine the outcome. This time they were on a mission—a noble, historic mission, as far as they were concerned. In fact, I could not remember a time when so many supposedly objective reporters had acted so blatantly as full-fledged advocates for one side—and without even a hint of embarrassment.

Other academic studies dismiss claims of liberal bias in the news because the content does not suggest it (e.g. Covert and Wasburn 2007). Others dismiss claims of liberal bias, arguing that to claim that journalists' preferences affect news content is akin to saying that the cook's preferences at McDonald's affect the menu. Such arguments do not dispute the existence of bias in the news, only its course and ideological direction. Because journalists are dependent upon owners and managers for their jobs, journalists are compelled to report stories that favor their bosses' supposedly economic elitist and conservative point of view (Chomsky 2006; Herman and Chomsky 1988). As leftist media critic Eric Alterman (2003) titles chapter 2 of *What Liberal Media? The Truth about Bias and the News*, "You're Only as Liberal as the Man Who Owns You."

But, while there do exist several studies on the topic, news bias has not been a major research trajectory for social scientists. This is shocking given popular concerns about it. This may be a problem of vantage point: academics are as liberal as, if not more liberal than, journalists. Academics would therefore not view liberally tilted news as tilted at all. Therefore, the notion of liberal media bias has not been given the attention in academia that many might think it warrants.

Scholars have presented evidence favoring these aforementioned top-down models; content analyses of news demonstrate that at times journalists favor our system of economics over others, focus on government accounts of events, and exhibit various forms of ideological bias. However, the evidence is often weak, or at best anecdotal. And more importantly, the majority of these studies do not account for the role of markets in shaping content. For example, as McManus (1995:332) argues, "While certain elites—major investors and the managers who put their wishes into practice—may exercise significant control over news content, they must appeal to a mass audience and often appear to do so by showing other parts of the establishment in a negative light." In other words, while supply-side models predict that news reports will always present leaders, corporations, and the system in a positive light, this is not the case. Outlets often report very negative stories about our institutions and leaders, economic, political, and otherwise. So, not only does the content often not match the predictions of elite-driven models, but the causal arrows are incorrectly specified: owners show negative portrayals of the system precisely because they are dependent on audiences. In other words, firm owners do not control the masses.

Also, the studies providing support for these models generally lack clear causal attribution. There is little evidence directly attributing news coverage to capitalist elites, government officials, or journalists and owners. News content can come about for a variety of reasons, and those arguing in favor of supply-side models have yet to demonstrate that a supply-side actor causes that content, except in limited subject areas or specific outlets (e.g. Puglisi and Snyder 2008; Chomsky 1999).

In short, supply-side models fail to explain the content of news because they are disconnected from the realities of markets. Economic elites, government officials, and newspeople can exhibit only so much control over news content before audiences turn away. Imagine an outlet that produces news content to advocate a particular point of view at the expense of consumer tastes. Audiences would stop consuming news from that outlet and choose instead to receive their news from another source (or perhaps choose to stop receiving news altogether). Unless this outlet could appeal to a large enough segment of the audience to remain viable, it would probably reorganize or go out of business.

Many might point to the left-leaning MSNBC or the right-leaning Fox News Channel as evidence that firms do actively bias their coverage. But, news producers are unable in the long run to propagandize or bias their news without, first, a demand for that particular style of content. So, while news outlets have their own detectable biases and styles, the demands of a segmented market, rather than the dispositions of journalists/owners/government officials or the secret cartel arrangements of capitalist elites, are the likely cause of that content.

Demand-Side Models

Demand-side (or bottom-up/audience-driven) models center on economics and contend that audience demand drives news firms. If a news firm did not need revenue to stay in business, then audience demand might have little say over content. Firms could report any story they want any way they want, without economic reprisal—the size of the audience would matter little. However, in the United States news firms must self-fund (or else eventually go out of business). This requires the capture of a large enough audience for the firm to profit from either sales of copy or sales of advertising. And, as public demands for news change over time, news firms have incentive to alter their products to meet those demands. In short, demand-side models account for the economic system.

News firms can account for a variety of audience demands: I group these demands into three types: entertainment, information, and gratification. These demands are not necessarily exclusive; the same content can satisfy two or more of these demands simultaneously. For example, an entertaining story can also meet audience demands for important pertinent information. I describe these three types of demands below, beginning with entertainment.

ENTERTAINMENT

Perhaps the most criticized aspect of news coverage is that audience demands have driven news outlets to make the news more "entertaining." Demands for entertainment may affect the content and quality of news as well as the aesthetics of news delivery. Furthermore, audience demands have led to more programming choices overall, so that people interested in entertainment need not be stuck watching the evening news (hundreds of other options are now available); this in itself has led to wide gaps in citizen knowledge and participation (Prior 2005). In terms of the content and quality of news, scholars have noted that much public affairs programming focuses on shocking, out-of-the-ordinary, and bizarre events. Scholars argue that this type of coverage is designed specifically to draw in and entertain audiences (Turrow 1983; Hamilton 1998). By reporting stories in this way, as opposed to stories that may better serve the public interest, audiences are left without pertinent information. For instance, a news outlet might provide minute-by-minute updates on Lindsay Lohan's criminal problems at the expense of covering proposed national crime legislation alternatives (Slattery et al. 2001).

In addition to ignoring more pertinent information, by meeting audience demands for entertainment, firms may also provide a twisted view of reality to audiences. For example, the summer of 2001 has oft been referred to as "summer of the shark." This is the case because reports of shark attacks had become frequent in the news, even though shark attacks that summer were not only infinitesimally rare but also on historic decline. But with this said, since people find "the idea of being eaten by a predator to be a shocking and outrageous way to die," shark attacks receive headlines while "deaths from modern ailments—from cardiovascular disease, cancer or infection—rarely rate a mention, and certainly don't get reported worldwide" (Dean 2010). In short, shark attack stories draw in audiences; cancer deaths do not. The increased shark coverage distorted reality, and as a result, irrationally amplified the fear of shark attacks and frightened summer vacationers away from the East Coast (McComas 2006).

To name one more recent example, in May 2012, a man stripped naked and attacked a homeless person, eating his eyeballs, nose, and mouth. Upon arriving at the scene, police shot the assailant ten times before he stopped the attack. Because the incident contained elements making it savory for audiences—nudity, bizarre behavior, mutilation, shooting, and death—the media immediately gave it prominent and sustained coverage; they termed it a "zombie" attack. The local and national media, without any toxicology reports, began attributing the attack to synthetic hallucinogenic drugs. The story became extremely salient in the weeks following, and still without a toxicology report, local governments as well as Congress began to react by banning, or further enforcing bans, on synthetic drugs.[8] Of course, getting attacked by a "zombie" on synthetic drugs, like getting eaten by a shark, is incredibly rare, but its inherent gruesomeness brings it heightened attention, skewing people's and government's perceptions of risk and priorities.

Scholars have been well aware that audience demands for entertainment bleed into political coverage, crowding out substantive policy discussion (Patterson 1994). Campaign coverage focuses on scandalous details of the candidate's past, the "shocking" new poll numbers, candidate gaffes, and discussions of campaign strategy (Farnsworth and Lichter 2010). For example, horse race coverage of presidential campaigns has trumped policy coverage on the networks in five of the last six elections, and usually by wide margins (Farnsworth and Lichter 2011). Entering the 2012 Republican presidential primaries, coverage focused on the results of numerous polls and on candidate strategy. Which Republican candidate has the most name recognition? Who can win what state? Who can win the nomination? Entering the 2012 general election, coverage focused on the horse race between Mitt Romney and Barack Obama. Who will win what state? Which campaign strategy is working? What do the latest polls say? This style of horse-race coverage adds little to public understanding of the issues at stake, and in a broader sense perverts the public's view of politics—people have begun to view analysis of campaign strategy as "good" coverage of politics (Iyengar et al. 2004). By focusing on questions such as these, outlets ignore more substantive questions, such as, How will the candidate govern if elected? What are the candidate's proposed policies, and how do those differ from the other candidates'? What will the effect of those espoused policies be? Beyond excluding more substantive and informative stories, this coverage leaves audiences with a jaded view of government: that leaders care only about strategic maneuvering, rather than making good policy. This may lead, in turn, to lower levels of trust in government and lower voter participation (Cappella and Jamieson 1996).

Beyond substantive news content, studies have long shown that news firms appeal to audience preferences for entertainment by altering the aesthetic (or nonsubstantive) aspects of the product. This might involve altering the background, the graphics, the music, or the delivery of the product. For newspapers, this might involve a greater use of colorful photos and graphics to convey information (*USA Today* has built its readership on such graphics). For televised news, this may involve scrolling tickers at the bottom of the screen, or picture-in-picture shots. This may also involve employing reporters who can attract audiences (Allen 1995). For example, the Fox News Network has developed a reputation for employing highly attractive females to anchor and comment on the news.

In terms of the press's journalistic obligations, meeting aesthetic demands is perhaps the least alarming. Assuming that the reporters are of equal competence, whether the news is delivered by attractive women such as Megan Kelly or by the less physically attractive Wolf Blitzer, the reporting is the same. Therefore, meeting demands for an aesthetically pleasing product does not necessarily deprive the audience. The problem occurs only when the aesthetics overtake or crowd out the substantive coverage (and therefore, I will not spend much time discussing this). Social scientists have had difficulty systematically measuring demands for entertainment, given that such demands are generally driven by subconscious psychological desires. Given this, it has been difficult for scholars to correlate changes in the levels of entertainment in the news to changes in demand for entertainment. This book operates under the assumption that audience demands for entertaining content are fairly constant. With this said, I would also claim that what is deemed entertaining or not will change over time.

INFORMATIONAL

A second form of demand for news involves the desire for specific information. Audiences may want to know more about a particular topic, or they may want a topic to receive more attention so that it can find resolution—journalists may respond to these demands by reporting the desired substantive information. Studies show that journalists do follow informational demands in this way. Audience concerns over a variety of issues, including Economics, the Environment, Civil Rights, Energy, Foreign Trade, and Social Welfare, have been shown to drive subsequent coverage of those issues in particular outlets at particular times (Behr and Iyengar 1985; Blood and Phillips 1997; Trumbo 1995). This can be viewed as a form of "civic-minded" journalism (Baker 2002:154-63). For instance, if the audience were to become highly concerned with the environment, then news firms would provide news addressing the environment. This form of civic-minded journalism is advocated by many as an important facet of democracy that increases news relevancy and can refocus government priorities (Bennett 2009). For example, at the local level, audiences may encourage more coverage of the local school board as opposed to coverage of car chases and convenience store stabbings.

While providing a public good, civic-minded journalism could lead to higher profits because firms would be meeting audience demands (Rosenstiel et al. 2007). While meeting informational demands in this way has its accolades, it also presents disadvantages. When journalists allow audiences to dictate substantive news content, they abdicate at least a portion of their independent judgment. In short, journalists should retain the ability to judge whether the audience's informational demands are worthy of precious news space. For example, audiences might develop a fascination with a politician's haircut. Journalists should be free to ignore those demands for information about the haircut and focus instead on the politician's espoused policies. Chapters 2 and 3 of this book will examine how information demands influence substantive coverage in traditional news sources.

GRATIFICATION

Beyond following demands for entertainment and information, news outlets may also follow demands for gratification (Katz et al. 1974). In this, audiences seek out news that accords with their ideological predispositions. For example, conservative audiences might turn to news sources that provide conservative news while liberals might turn to news sources that provide liberal news. According to studies of the current ideologically segmented news market, audiences do in fact self-select into like-minded news programs: conservatives self-select to receive news from Fox News while more liberal viewers self-select into watching CNN or MSNBC (Morris 2007). These outlets have benefited greatly from targeting segments of the ideologically diverse audience, and their experience shows that news firms indeed have incentive to provide comforting rather than challenging news.

In meeting demands for gratification, firms do not necessarily provide news that meets a specific demand for pertinent information or a demand for nonsubstantive entertainment (although they could). Rather, outlets supply agreeable news that meets psychological needs for reassurance and value reinforcement (McQuail 1987). By relying on agreeable news, consumers wind up with different perceptions of reality than the rest of the news audience (Morris 2007). This leaves audiences without a broad, unbiased view of the major events and issues.

Many are well acquainted with the idea that media firms target certain demographic groups. For example, newspapers may target homeowners; televised programs may target particular age groups. This may seem rather innocuous, until one considers more fully that these demographics dictate the substantive aspects of news content. Recent studies show that in local news sources, coverage of a variety of topics, including campaigns (Cardwell 2005), gay rights (Pollock et al. 2006b), Islam (Pollock et al. 2005), and immigration (Branton and Dunaway 2009), varies according to the demographics of local audiences. In other words, many news outlets attempt to present news that accords with what the audience already believes—even though this news may provide a false picture of reality.

Despite the growing body of evidence, many disagree about the role of demands for gratification in determining content. For example, Entman (2005:54) argues that in the more traditional news organizations, "decisions to cover stories, how to play them, how much to follow up, and the like are made more on grounds of professional news judgment than on immediate profit calculations." In addition, in studying newspaper content, Puglisi and Snyder (2011) and Larcinese et al. (2007) find that news outlets do not follow the political tastes of audiences, except in limited instances. In fact, they find that newspapers are more likely to follow the ideological dispositions of the editors than of the audiences. To settle this disagreement in the literature and also better specify the effects of demands for gratification on content, chapters 3 and 4 will explore the impact of audience demands for gratification to see how much these demands affect news content as well as the news landscape. To conclude this section, explanations of news content can be organized into three major paradigms: traditional journalism, supply-side, and demand-side. I argue that demand-side arguments provide the best explanation for news content. There are three basic demands consumers may have for news: demands for entertainment, for information, and for gratification. The remaining chapters of this book will present evidence in favor of demand-side economic models of news content.

Plan of the Book

The People's News proceeds as follows. Chapter 2 begins discussion and critique of the media-effects literature. Then, it segues into a presentation of the data analyzed in chapters 2 and 3. This data comes from the three nightly network news programs. Chapter 2 then employs time-series analysis to demonstrate how audience demands for information determine, in many instances, substantive issue coverage in the news. Chapter 3 looks at how news firms meet audience demands for gratification by following the audience's ideological and partisan preferences. The chapter examines both cable and broadcast news programming to determine whether and how the audience's ideology and partisanship affect the market structure and substantive content of news. Taken together, chapters 2 and 3 show how audience demands for information and gratification lead even supposedly "traditional" news firms to alter substantive content in response.

Chapter 4 begins by delineating the methods with which news firms can more efficiently than ever track audience preferences and respond immediately with content that meets those preferences. Then, chapter 4 provides examples of news firms adjusting coverage before and after polls, showing stark contrasts to what was previously thought about public opinion. With this, chapter 4 demonstrates that the public can immediately affect the coverage certain topics receive.

Given the findings of audience influence over news content in chapters 2, 3, and 4, it seems as though the U.S. media environment offers society the worst-case scenario: a dire need for an independent media that cannot be independent. Chapter 5 places the book's empirical findings into perspective, arguing that popular notions of independence and objectivity have created a "witch-hunt" for ideological bias, thus obscuring the larger forces affecting news: economics. To conclude, chapter 5 asks, What are the potential solutions? Given the sweeping changes occurring in all levels and mediums of news, this discussion touches on the future of news content, election outcomes, policy decisions, and, in general, democratic governance in the United States. In the end, I discuss whether democracy can survive when the information necessary to democratic decision making is discarded in favor of what sells.

Conclusion

In the United States, news outlets have unique protections that are unprecedented in most of the world. The reason for these protections is that self-rule relies on ample sources of independent information. Without ample independent information, citizens cannot make informed or rational decisions as voters, they cannot attend to the important problems that call for resolution, and they cannot hold leaders to account for their actions. In short, American democracy calls upon the news media to be *the* source of independent information. This responsibility is unfortunately aggravated by the incentives built into the American economic system. News firms, despite the unique protections they enjoy, must still operate like any other type of firm. This means that news outlets must incur a profit or go out of business. Scholars have long noted that economic incentives drive much of the news industry, from the opening and closing of foreign bureaus to the corporatization and conglomeration of many of the current outlets. However, scholars have arrived at less of a consensus about how much economics affect the *substantive* content of news. This book seeks to better determine how much market demands aggravate the demands of democratic citizenship. In undertaking this task, this book will not only shed light on the construction of the news but also lead to a greater understanding of how the media meet their responsibilities to democratic governance. To this end, chapter 2 examines how demands for information influence not only the content of news but also the ability of the news to influence the public and its leaders.

2

Informational Demands for News

Agenda Setting and Audience Influence

Well, news is anything that's interesting, that relates to what's
happening in the world, what's happening in areas of the culture that would be of interest to your audience.
—Kurt Loder, 1994

What is news? What makes a piece of information newsworthy? Perhaps it is something inherent in a piece of information that sets it apart
from millions of pieces of other information—perhaps the people *need*
to know it for society to function properly. Or, perhaps information
becomes newsworthy because of the way audience members would
individually value that piece of information. In the former instance,
information can have inherent value regardless of whether the audience
chooses to value it, consume it, or demand it—the information serves
a greater good. In the latter, the value of a piece of information comes
from audience interest and demand. It is little surprise that Kurt Loder,
a journalist who spent most of his career working for the entertainment
outlets *Rolling Stone Magazine* and MTV, would equate news with the
audience's interest. The outlets Loder spent most of his journalism career
working for have no responsibility to inform or cultivate democratic

society; the news they cover is there to entertain. The bigger question is, Do journalists at more traditional news sources view news as information that meets a public demand, or as information serving something larger and more systemic? This chapter sets out to answer that question.

Chapter 1 introduced the tension between democratic ideals and economic necessities. While democratic societies require robust sources of information to make far-reaching policy decisions, the marketplace for news, on the other hand, requires large enough audiences so that outlets can be profitable. The need for news outlets to incur profits may lead them to shirk their responsibilities to democratic society. Outlets may therefore provide news that brings in audiences by meeting their demands but does not encourage informed decision making in matters of public importance. Chapter 1 also introduced three types of audience demand that news firms may follow: demands for information, for entertainment, and for gratification. This chapter examines the way demands for information affect the amount of coverage given to broad, substantive issue areas over time.

A great deal of evidence has been amassed suggesting that the news media greatly impact the public's political opinions and behaviors. Chapter 1 provided the broad strokes of these arguments. Perhaps the most broadly accepted and studied impact of the news is its ability to set the audience's issue agenda. In this scenario, news outlets report issues, and the public subsequently views those issues as important. This represents a very powerful effect, and a multitude of studies have lent credence to this paradigm, called "agenda-setting." The seminal study, performed by Maxwell McCombs and Donald Shaw, showed that the issues reported in the news during the 1968 presidential campaign strongly *correlated* with the issues that were salient with audiences (McCombs and Shaw 1972).

With this said, correlations between the media's agenda and the public's agenda do not necessarily indicate that the media have set the audience's agenda. A correlation between two numerical variables implies only that their values rise and fall in relation to one another; correlation does not imply that one variable *causes* the other. A correlation between issue coverage in the news and the public perception of issue importance may indicate that the news influences the public, or instead that public demand for issue coverage drives news content. A correlation between news and public opinion may also indicate that news firms and the audience both respond to the same stimuli, but are not causally related. A correlation may even exist if news content and audiences are not related at all. In short, correlation between news content and public opinion may indicate more than one relationship between news and the public.

Given this observational equivalency, and the economic incentives that drive news outlets to provide news that meets audience demand, it is possible that in the past scholars overestimated the impact that news outlets have on the public's agenda and at the same time underestimated the impact that audience demands have on news content. In this chapter, I explain how audience demands affect news issue content and therefore mediate the agenda-setting impact that news outlets could potentially have on audiences.

This chapter proceeds as follows. First, I briefly detail the history of media effects research to show that researchers have studied the media with an eye towards identifying media effects (rather than identifying evidence of audience influence). Second, I critique the studies of agenda setting to show how both methodological and theoretical limitations in the literature may have led scholars to overestimate the causal impact between the media's and the public's agendas. Building from these critiques, I then design an analysis to compare the issues reported in the nightly network news to data measuring public concern over a period of forty years. The results of this statistical analysis suggest that audiences have a strong and meaningful influence over news content. I conclude with implications for the study of media effects and for journalism.

The Study of Media Effects

Social scientists have taken a keen interest in the news media for nearly a century; however, much of the attention paid to the news has focused on its influence over audiences, specifically mass political opinions and behaviors. This interest was widely sparked after World Wars I and II (e.g. Lasswell 1927). In trying to understand how otherwise rational and compassionate human beings could actively support the horrors of brutal totalitarian regimes, researchers looked to their propaganda machines. Scientists concluded that film and print propaganda must have had a powerful effect in achieving compliance and active participation (Smith et al. 1946). This line of thought motivated what became known as the "hypodermic needle" theory (Bineham 1988). According to this theory, audiences immediately absorb media messages; these messages then alter the audience's political preferences (Chaffee and Hochheimer 1985). Radio messages extolling the virtues of Benito Mussolini would lead listeners to support Benito Mussolini just as Nazi propaganda films would lead viewers to support Hitler. This theory provides both a powerful and a parsimonious explanation not only for the opinions and behavior of people in authoritarian regimes but also for public opinion writ large. However, some strong assumptions are written into the hypodermic needle theory—first, that audiences' opinions are extremely fungible and, second, that audiences are captive and choose to absorb any content provided them.

Beginning in the 1930s, Paul Lazarsfeld and his team conducted a series of county-wide panel studies in the northeastern United States during election seasons (e.g. Lazarsfeld et al. 1944; see also Berelson et al. 1954; Katz and Lazarsfeld 1955; Klapper 1960). Their goal was to observe, through a series of repeated interviews, how media messages (news and advertisements) affected audience preference for political candidates, fashion, entertainment, and household products. In short, they wanted to test the veracity of the hypodermic needle theory. They surmised that if the theory was accurate, they would observe an ebb and flow of public preferences closely following the ebb and flow of media messages. What they found instead shaped the study of media effects forever.

The findings showed no strong evidence to support a hypodermic effect: regardless of the amount or type of exposure to news and advertisements, voter preferences changed little in the months leading up to elections. With little evidence to support it, researchers tossed aside the hypodermic needle theory and continued the search for and the effort to develop better theories to understand how the media influence the public (Katz 1987).

Shortly thereafter, researchers at the University of Michigan published *The American Voter* (Campbell et al. 1960), perhaps the most cited work in the field of political science. This exhaustive work's most important contribution is in showing the stability of people's political opinions. The findings indicated that people's political opinions arise from processes embedded in socialization and are, for the most part, impervious to external stimuli such as news and advertising (see also Campbell et al. 1966; Campbell et al. 1954). Thus, opinions such as political ideology, policy preferences, and partisan attachments were stable not only over the course of months or campaign seasons but also over the course of lifetimes. Because of the stability introduced by socialization and other social-psychological processes, there was little room for media messages to affect opinions. This gave support to a "minimal effects" model of media influence that became the conventional wisdom for decades (Chaffee and Hochheimer 1985).

The minimal effects model relies on two basic claims. First, audiences have an active resistance to messages that challenge their partisan attachments, political ideology, or policy preferences. Audiences will either ignore or overly scrutinize information with which they disagree (Klapper 1960). This indicates a psychological resistance to discordant media messages. With audiences ignoring information that could change their current opinions, the media are left with little room to affect audiences. News messages therefore serve to reinforce existing opinions, but not to change them. Second, and perhaps more importantly, audiences self-select media sources that meet their demands, while at the same time avoiding news sources that do not. One cannot be influenced by a news source if one chooses not to consume it. By positing these two levels of resistance, the minimal effects model began to account for the impact of audience's predispositions and choices on the ability of the media to affect audiences.

Suspecting that the effect of mass media in shaping opinions was vastly underestimated in the minimal effects paradigm, in the late 1960s

scientists reexamined the link between news content and audience opinions. Using previously untested conjecture as a starting point (Lippman
1922; Lang and Lang 1966; Cohen 1963), researchers argued that while
the media might not affect what audiences think, they could affect what
audiences think *about*. This became known as the "agenda-setting"
hypothesis. Maxwell McCombs and Donald Shaw, in the first direct test
of agenda-setting, surveyed undecided voters in North Carolina during
the 1968 presidential election (McCombs and Shaw 1972). Subjects were
asked to state the issues that they felt were the most important. They
compared these with the frequency with which those issues were discussed in the news and found that the public's ranking of issue salience
closely matched issue salience in the news. This provided the first
empirical evidence of the media's "agenda-setting" power, and a long
series of studies in the ensuing decades buttressed the original findings
by McCombs and Shaw (see McCombs 2004 for a synopsis of many of
these studies).

In the 1980s, political scientists sought to strengthen support for the
agenda-setting hypothesis using experimental conditions. In a laboratory setting, Iyengar et al. (1982) showed subjects a manipulated news
program and then asked them to identify what they thought the most
important issues were. The subjects subsequently identified the issues
highlighted in the news programming as the most important; this provided strong support for the agenda-setting hypothesis. Experiments
such as this are said to provide the "best, most unequivocal evidence"
of agenda-setting because, unlike in many observational designs, laboratory settings are able to isolate the direction of causal influence—in
this case from the news "treatment" to the subject's ranking of issue
salience (McCombs 2004:17). Because the researchers construct the
news "treatment," experimental designs can rule out (1) the possibility
that the news was following the subjects' preferences and (2) the possibility that both the news and the subjects were responding to the same
stimuli.

As a whole, the correlations between the public agenda and the media
agenda found in both observational and experimental studies provide

fairly convincing support for the agenda-setting hypothesis. The wealth of evidence led to a paradigm shift in the study of media: media effects came to be understood in the social sciences within the agenda-setting paradigm (McCombs 2004).

Critiques of Agenda-Setting

Despite the wealth of evidence supporting the agenda-setting paradigm (hundreds of studies have been produced), social scientists have frequently pointed to design flaws that may lead researchers to overestimate the impact of the media's agenda on audiences and underestimate the impact that audiences have on the news agenda. Beginning with the seminal work by McCombs and Shaw, researchers often acknowledged the possibility that the audience's opinions drove the news agenda; however, these alternative views were initially rejected (1972:185):

> Interpreting the evidence from this study as indicating mass media influence seems more plausible than alternative explanations. Any argument that the correlations between media and voter emphasis are spurious— that they are simply responding to the same events and not influencing each other one way or the other—assumes that voters have alternative means of observing the day-to-day changes in the political arena. This assumption is not plausible; since few directly participate in presidential election campaigns, and fewer still see presidential candidates in person, the information flowing in interpersonal communication channels is primarily relayed from, and based upon, mass media news coverage. The media are the major primary sources of national political information; for most, mass media provide the best—and only—easily available approximation of ever-changing political realities. It might also be argued that the high correlations indicate that the media simply were successful in matching their messages to audience interests. Yet since numerous studies indicate a sharp divergence between the news values of professional journalists and their audiences, it would be remarkable to find a near perfect fit in this one case.

The above argument indicates the willingness of media-effects researchers to give heightened deference to the notion that the media influences the public. To take both of the arguments laid out by McCombs and Shaw above, first, it is entirely possible that news organizations and audiences respond to the same cues. For instance, if gas prices increase, the media report it; but people also feel the pain at the pump first-hand as well. Those paying five dollars per gallon need not be told by journalists that prices are high. Second, if news organizations value having audiences, making money, and staying in business, then it is entirely possible that news will hew closely to audience opinions and demands. Sincerity is a much overrated virtue. Regardless of whether or not journalists share political values with audiences, their personal values are irrelevant. News firms have the means and an overarching incentive to follow audience demands.

Early agenda-setting studies were undertaken specifically to find a causal effect from media to audience (McCombs 2004:4; Behr and Iyengar 1985:40). As a result, the agenda-setting literature, for several years, made little effort to integrate market forces into its expectations. Beginning with the early observational studies, which rely on cross-sectional correlations between public salience and media salience (e.g. Funkhouser 1973), researchers automatically interpreted correlations between the news agenda and the public agenda as indicating not only that they were causally related but also that the causal arrow pointed from news content to audience. As Behr and Iyengar (1985:40) argued of the extant literature, "It is taken for granted that news coverage is the driving force and that agenda-setting is a unidirectional . . . process. The possibility of a feedback effect, namely, that public concern itself spawns news coverage, is ignored."

As computing power increased and social-scientific methods diversified, subsequent researchers employed sophisticated statistical techniques that could account for dual causation between media salience and public salience in observational studies. However, even these studies assumed a causal direction from media to audience, and consequently, they were designed to examine the effect of media over the public rather than to investigate the effect of the public on the media. These studies were rarely designed to present a fair test between the competing conceptions of audience influence over the news and media influence over the audience: the research designs, including the units of time, topics, and data collection efforts, generally focused on identifying agenda-setting effects while making only minimal effort to rule out other potential causes of correlation. For example, studies examined news coverage of narrow topics that are perhaps reported to satisfy audience demands for coverage of broader areas. For example, some studies focus on topics such as the Gulf War, natural disasters, industrial accidents, and school shootings (Birkland 1998; Chyi and McCombs 2004; Iyengar and Simon 1993). When researchers pick such narrow topics to study, results will naturally bias in favor of finding an agenda-setting effect. This is the case because citizens cannot know about specific, narrow, or geographically limited events before they occur; therefore, the only possible direction of influence is from news outlet to audience. If a school burns down in Wichita, Kansas, it would be nearly impossible for the masses of people in New Hampshire to know about it without a news outlet telling them first. If we were to compare concern over the Wichita incident to coverage of it, only an agenda-setting effect can occur.

Such a scenario may also occur if news outlets give disproportionate coverage to a topic, or report on events that are not occurring. For example, in March 2012, ABC ran a series of stories about a type of meat termed "pink slime." Few people had ever heard of or cared about the meat deemed "pink slime" at that point, but, because of the news stories, people became concerned about the health effects of eating it. The meat was perfectly healthy and had exhibited no harmful effects, so there was little reason in the real world for people to be concerned. But, because of the specious reporting, people immediately became concerned, and orders for that type of meat plummeted. The media can easily set the public's agenda if one conceptualizes the effect in these narrow terms.

One way to put this into perspective is to consider that the public could have a preexisting demand that coverage of specific events satisfies. Outlets may in fact respond to those broader demands, but studies looking only at the specific coverage may find significant influence of that specific coverage on opinion while missing the broader influence of audience demands that drove the coverage in the first place. For instance, if the public became broadly interested in food safety, then news outlets might provide more coverage of food manufacturers violating safety standards. Coverage of these specific instances would then increase knowledge, awareness, and concern regarding those specific instances. But in the end, the public was already concerned with food—so news reports were responding to that concern.

Despite the fact that many agenda-setting studies were not designed to look for these broader audience influences, studies repeatedly found evidence suggesting that on occasion, the audience sets the issue agenda for the media (see Rogers and Dearing 2007). For example, studies showed that audience concerns over inflation (Behr and Iyengar 1985), economic recession (Blood 1996; Blood and Phillips 1997; Stevenson et al. 1991), the environment (Trumbo 1995), and community issues (Smith 1987b) drove news coverage of those issues.

On one hand, studies showing audience influence could simply be statistical artifacts. The real world is a complicated and messy place, rife with instances that defy clear theoretical explanation. But, on the other hand, if these repeated findings are not artifacts, then we do not know the extent of audience influence over news content. In other words, what is the effect of the media over the audience, and what is the effect of the audience over the media? What can we say about these two opposing forces more generally?

Studies in the laboratory unequivocally show that the news media have an "uncanny capacity" to set the agenda for the audience (Behr and Iyengar 1985:39; Iyengar et al. 1982). Unfortunately, while the controlled conditions allow for isolation of the causal treatment, they manipulate reality in such a way as to lose external validity. In other words, the controlled conditions of the laboratory do not replicate the processes taking place in reality. Therefore, it is reasonable to question whether experiments showing evidence of agenda-setting indicate processes taking place in the real world.

The investigators purposefully choose the news programming without regard for drawing in an audience. Of course, this is how experiments work: researchers choose stimuli without much regard for the subjects' particular tastes. Because these designs ignored the incentives for news firms to follow audience demands as well as the fact that audiences self-select the news they prefer, the results may have greatly overestimated the potential for news firms to impact audiences in the field. Thus, laboratory studies only investigated one-half of the media-audience relationship.

Researchers, responding to the limitations inherent in past experimental work, have recently introduced the element of audience choice into laboratory studies of media effects (e.g. Arceneaux and Johnson 2010; Arceneaux et al. 2012). Findings indicate that when subjects are held less captive and allowed to choose their programming, as they would in the real world, opinions are far more stable and the media's ability to influence audience opinions is significantly diminished (see also Druckman et al. 2012).

On one hand, the agenda-setting framework argues that the media influence the audience's assessment of issue salience. On the other hand, economic theories argue that the audience's demands for specific sets of information should drive informational content in the news. Researchers have amassed theory and evidence supporting both points of view; however, the extant literature does not adequately adjudicate between these two opposing arguments. I now present a test employing a long time frame, longer units of time than are typically employed, and broad, substantive issue areas. This should provide a fair test for both agenda-setting and audience influence over the news. When an isolated event occurs, few people know about it because most people are effectively isolated from events not in their immediate vicinity. Thus, when the media inform people about the event, the only possible direction for effects is from media to audience. It would be impossible for people to know about a remote event before it happened and demand that it be reported on.

With broader issue areas, however, the audience has the ability to think about those issues before the media reports isolated events falling within them. As a result, the public can possess a demand for coverage of a broad issue area, and the news media can respond by reporting stories that fit into it. News firms can be aware of issue demands, and respond accordingly. For example, if the public becomes concerned with the environment, outlets will follow by reporting stories about the environment to meet the demand for that information. Broad categories of coverage, therefore, allow a fair simultaneous test of audience influence and agenda-setting. When firms meet these demands, the public drives the news coverage.

To be clear on definitions, an issue involves "cumulative news coverage of a series of related events that fit together in a broad category" while an event is a "discrete happening that is limited by space and time" (Shaw 1977). For example, the issue of "Defense" would include all stories involving national defense, while an event might include today's troop battle in Afghanistan.

The following sections of this chapter provide empirical support for this argument. I begin by describing the dataset of news content that will be used in both this chapter and chapter 3. I then describe the measure I use to operationalize public demands for information: a time-series of responses to Gallup's Most Important Problem question. I then use time-series analysis to test the above framework.

Scope

To examine the influence of audiences on subsequent news content, I look to empirics. It is easy to claim that audiences drive news; it is much harder to amass actual evidence favoring the argument. This is where collecting and analyzing data comes in handy. With data, researchers can create a test for better understanding the relationship between the audience and the media. I begin by creating a time-series of news content. There are many outlets (local and national) and forms of news (televised, print, radio, and internet) that could be used to test the veracity of this chapter's claims. However, to provide a fair test, I employ stories from the three televised national broadcast news programs: ABC, CBS, and NBC.

While I employ data from these three networks, I acknowledge that news takes many forms and comes from thousands of different producers. It would be beyond the scope of one, or even several, books to collect and test data from all outlets of news. The best one can do is to focus on sources of data that are likely to present a fair test of the theories proffered and can be somewhat generalizable to other forms of news (even if with caveats). Consider this study like a road map: even though we lose some finer details, we can see the contours of the broader landscape. With this said, I will discuss other mediums, such as newspapers and the internet, where appropriate.

Let me elucidate why the broadcast networks are ideal for testing this chapter's (and later on, chapter 3's) theory. First, the broadcast networks deserve study because of the sheer size and scope of their audiences. These programs reach the entire country and are, by many, considered the elite news sources "of record." Because they are broadcast nationally, each of the three broadcast news shows consistently beat all of the cable news shows in terms of audience size. In the late 1960s, the networks had about fifty-five million viewers per broadcast. Network dominance was due in part to a near-monopoly until cable networks began prominently competing in the 1980s. Partially due to the emergence of cable, viewership declined 50 percent to about twenty-four million by 2009. However, the three broadcasts remain the largest draw of viewers during the time slot (Hamilton 2005). Thus, the broadcast news provides the opportunity to test this framework in a setting in which media effects may have pervasive consequences.

Second, while the networks are targeted by some as ideologically biased and untrustworthy (Goldberg 2002, 2009), the network news programs are established institutions with long-standing public trust (Miller and Krosnick 2000). This trust allows the programs to impact audiences' assessments of salience as people are likely to believe what they view (Eagly and Chaiken 1993). This makes them ideal for examining the influence of audience opinions over news.

Third, because of constitutional protections, the networks have discretion over their coverage; there are no government restrictions forcing news firms to report one story or another. Therefore, should the networks choose to adjust their coverage to follow public demands, they have few limitations in doing so. Along with constitutional protections, networks are private firms with incentive to increase profits and audience size. Perhaps the only restriction the networks have is that they must maintain large enough audiences to stay in business. Other than this, the networks can adjust their programming as they see fit.

Fourth, the networks have the tools necessary to follow audience demands. Networks are large organizations with huge staffs, marketing departments, and offices dedicated to following ratings; they are aware of the percentage of the potential audience watching their own and others' programming. Networks commission their own polls and have access to a vast array of audience information (such as extensive Nielsen data). Chapter 4 will expand on this point further.

Fifth, practicality makes the use of network news ideal. The content from these news sources has been catalogued for decades and is readily available for study. Also, given that the programs are national, they correspond to measures of national public opinion (state- and local-level opinions are less readily available than national measures). This allows the use of longitudinal analysis because national public opinion measures have been taken at regular intervals for the last several decades.

Finally, the nightly network news provides a difficult test for finding evidence of audience influence. This is the case because there is less of an expectation that the networks, as opposed to other outlets, will follow audience demands. The nightly network broadcasts are widely considered "traditional" news sources (Entman 2005:54; see also Fengler and Russ-Mohl 2008). Thus, of the many news sources available for this study, the nightly network news provides a more difficult and therefore *fair* test of audience influence.[1]

The news data are derived from the Vanderbilt Media Archive, which has abstracts of the broadcasts going back to August 1968. Included in this are descriptions and summaries of each story appearing in the broadcasts.[2] Because the archive contains *abstracts* of the stories, rather than the entirety of each story, scholars have been concerned about its ability to accurately represent the content of each story. But, this appears a minor concern for current purposes—findings indicate that the abstracts are appropriate in the aggregate and contain enough detail for this current study (Althaus et al. 2002). During the period from August 5, 1968, to March 31, 2010, 64,747 stories were coded.[3] The 42-year time frame provides adequate variation from which to draw conclusions: it encompasses nine presidencies, periods of war and peace, and varying levels of economic prosperity.

The dataset includes the first two stories from each weekday broadcast from the three networks. It is important to examine the process leading to the selection of the top two stories for two reasons. First, the networks may attempt to attract viewers at the beginning of the program, not unlike the way newspapers use headlines. If networks were attempting to attract audiences, this should be observed most acutely in the top stories. Second, the media-effects literature suggests that audiences judge the importance of particular stories by their placement within the broadcast (McCombs 2004). Those appearing at the beginning, sometimes explicitly denoted as "top stories," have the most impact on the public's perception of issue salience. In short, in simultaneously testing the agenda-setting and audience-driven theories, this data provides a fair test.

Despite the reasons for focusing on these stories, some may be concerned that using only the top two stories may induce bias into the analysis. To ease these concerns, I collected a second sample of stories from the entirety of the programs over the time frame. The issue distribution in the entirety of the programs mirrors that in the top two stories, and an analysis of the stories from the entirety of the programs buttresses the results summarized in chapters 2 and 3. In short, the stories aired at the top of the programs are little different from the remainder of the programs.

There are many facets of news that can be examined: length of story, placement of story, tone of the story, etc. I do not examine length because the program structure packages stories into similar lengths. Therefore, there isn't wide variation. I do not include a measure of tone/spin in this analysis because there is no clear theoretical expectation about how tone would be applied and what issues it would be applied to—and furthermore, it is not clear that the Vanderbilt abstracts could be used to discern tone validly. In general, coding for tone is performed on campaign stories because it is a fairly straightforward matter to discern tone not only from the style of reporting but also from the event being reported.

The framework in this chapter refers to *issue* coverage. This is appropriate because the agenda-setting literature contends that it is the *issue areas* (McCombs 2005), as opposed to other characteristics, such as spin, that affect public-issue salience. To reiterate, an issue involves "a series of related events that fit together in a broad category" while an event is a "discrete happening that is limited by space and time" (Shaw 1977). News firms provide news addressing isolated, singular events (Rogers and Dearing 2007). During the time period under study, the broadcast firms covered thousands of events, from Watergate hearings to domestic terror attacks. For practicality's sake, and to assemble stories into categories that might meet broad audience interests, it is appropriate to group news stories into a manageable number of substantive issue categories that can be tracked over a long period.

Content analysis is a method in which units are placed into categories. In this case, I code stories from the nightly network news by placing each story into a category; each category represents a broad issue area. The stories are coded according to the Baumgartner and Jones Policy Agendas issue scheme (Baumgartner and Jones 2006). This scheme codes subject matter into substantive categories and has been used frequently to code congressional hearings, executive orders, public opinion, and newspaper content (e.g. Baumgartner et al. 1997b). I use this scheme with only minor modifications. Table 2.1 shows the issue area categories, along with some examples of stories that fall into each area.

I separate the data into quarterly observations for both theoretical and practical purposes. The agenda-setting literature argues that audiences are most influenced by news when the same content is repeated over time (McCombs 2005). Thus, quarterly units of observation should adequately capture agenda-setting. Also, because this analysis examines

Table 2.1. Issue Areas and Example Stories

Issue Area Code Topics	Example
International Affairs	Diplomatic Visits, Negotiations, Foreign Disasters
Defense	War, Weapons, Military Maneuvers
Federal Government Operations	Government Scandals, Government Wrongdoing
Law, Crime	Crimes, Arrests, Trials
Macroeconomics	Stock Market Performance, Economic Indicators
Transportation	Road Maintenance
Health Issues	Medical Studies, Disease Control
Energy	Gas Shortages, Nuclear Power
Banking, Finance, and Domestic Commerce	Interest Rates, Loans, Domestic Business
Civil Rights	Marches, Legal Rights, Police Brutality, Race Riots
Space, Science, Technology, and Communications	Space Missions, Technological Advancements
Labor and Employment	Labor Disputes
Social Welfare	Social Security
Foreign Trade	Trade Regulations, Disputes
Environment	Conservation Programs, Pollution
Agriculture	Farm Subsidies
Education	Performance, Funding
Community Development and Housing	Housing Creation, Renovation
Public Lands and Water Management	Sale of Lands, Water Policy
Other, Miscellaneous	All Others, Elvis's Estate

the interplay between news content and media effects, it is advantageous to examine issue reporting over longer intervals so that public opinion has time to fluctuate and firms have time to fully react. Thus, the use of quarterly intervals is in line with what researchers know about news firms. While firms react on a nightly basis to events because they constantly occur, public opinions do not necessarily vary enough in the immediate term to warrant smaller units of time. Quarterly observations provide an average of 388 total stories per quarter.[4]

Table 2.2 begins with the frequency and percentage of each issue area in the dataset—these numbers speak to the three networks as a whole. This is followed by the percentage of the data falling into each issue. The

Table 2.2. Issue Area Frequencies and Percentages

Issue	Percent of Total (Frequency)
International Affairs	24% (15,683)
Defense	14% (9,644)
Federal Government Operations	10% (6,886)
Law, Crime	8% (5,274)
Macroeconomics	7% (4,832)
Transportation	2% (1,640)
Health Issues	2% (1,538)
Energy	2% (1,407)
Banking, Finance, and Domestic Commerce	2% (1,393)
Civil Rights	2% (1,196)
Space, Science, Technology, and Communications	115% (988)
Labor and Employment	1% (904)
Social Welfare	1% (880)
Foreign Trade	1% (635)
Environment	0.6% (389)
Agriculture	0.5% (298)
Education	0.3% (171)
Community Development and Housing	0.2% (124)
Public Lands and Water Management	0.0% (29)
Other, Miscellaneous	16.7% (10,823)

most frequently reported stories are those in the International Affairs category; these comprise 24 percent of the data. This is probably the case for a few reasons. First, International Affairs is a broad category—it includes events from the entire world. As a result, there is nearly unlimited geographic area to gather news from. Second, because the broadcast programs are national, they will inherently look at matters involving international relations because these stories address matters concerning the country as a whole.

While complaints have been aired in the past that the news media have insulated Americans from international news, this clearly seems not to be the case—at least in terms of the *amount* of news addressing international relations (American reporting of international news does have an Amero-centric slant to it). Stories about international affairs are aired ten percentage points more than the next most frequent category. The data do show, however, that International Affairs reporting by the three networks has dipped in recent years: this could be a result of declining revenues that have led to the closing of foreign news bureaus.

The second most frequently reported issue area is Defense; this issue comprises 15 percent of the data. Rounding out the top three is Federal Government Operations; this comprises 11 percent of the data. Again, given the national nature of the nightly network news, stories about national defense and the federal government are within the national scope of the broadcast programs. In addition, during the time period in question, four major wars have taken place (Cold War, Vietnam War, Iraq War, and War on Terror), along with several smaller conflicts—this has no doubt driven coverage of Defense. In addition, several major scandals have occurred at the national level that account for much of the coverage of Federal Government Operations, including Watergate, Iran-Contra, and the Clinton impeachment. These scandals appear to drive coverage of this issue. Coverage of Law & Crime and Macroeconomics round out the five most frequently reported issue areas; these are the only five issue areas above 5 percent. These two issues, like International Affairs and Defense, also address topics that are of importance to the nation as a whole.

Fourteen other issue areas occupy less than 5 percent of the data each; six of these occupy 1 percent or less. While it is telling to see which areas receive coverage, it is equally telling to see which areas receive little coverage. Public Lands & Water Management, Community Development and Housing, and Education each occupy less than half of 1 percent of the data. It is hard to imagine that these issues would be so unimportant to society that they collectively would only account for .5 percent of the news stories during a forty-two year span. This demonstrates the difference between issues that are of enduring importance to society and issues involving flashy events that draw in audiences. It is important to note that the distribution of issues in the nightly network news programs is not much different from the issue distribution in the *New York Times,* for example, or other major news outlets (Puglisi 2011; Shaw and Sparrow 1999).

A closer look at the news stories in table 2.3 demonstrates that the networks have nearly identical issue coverage. For example, in their coverage of International Affairs, they differ by less than 1 percent; in their coverage of Public Lands and Water Management, the networks differ by only one story. Therefore, the following analyses will combine coverage from ABC, CBS, and NBC into one robust measure of content. The similarity of the three networks comes as no surprise: studies consistently show that network news programs are very similar (McCombs 2004:116). This also suggests an audience-driven news media: if the three networks were using issue coverage to compete for the same audience, then we should expect them to have similar coverage.

One might wonder how the three networks compared to the cable news stations. Table 2.4 shows news stories from CNN as a comparison.

Table 2.3. Comparing Issue Coverage among Broadcasters

Issue	Frequency			Percent (%)		
	ABC	CBS	NBC	ABC	CBS	NBC
International Affairs	5,347	5,177	5,159	24.8	23.9	24.0
Defense	3,186	3,264	3,194	14.8	15.1	14.8
Federal Government Operations	2,248	2,332	2,306	10.4	10.8	10.7
Law, Crime	1,576	1,861	1,837	7.3	8.6	8.5
Macroeconomics	1,492	1,667	1,673	6.9	7.7	7.8
Transportation	509	541	590	2.4	2.5	2.7
Health Issues	559	500	479	2.6	2.3	2.2
Energy	462	512	433	2.1	2.4	2.0
Banking, Finance, and Domestic Commerce	470	458	468	2.2	2.1	2.2
Civil Rights	426	370	400	2.0	1.7	1.9
Space, Science, Technology, and Communications	331	354	303	1.5	1.6	1.4
Labor and Employment	236	315	353	1.1	1.5	1.6
Social Welfare	276	318	286	1.3	1.5	1.3
Foreign Trade	226	219	190	1.0	1.0	0.9
Environment	129	126	134	0.6	0.6	0.6
Agriculture	97	106	95	0.4	0.5	0.4
Education	76	38	57	0.4	0.2	0.3
Community Development and Housing	37	46	41	0.2	0.2	0.2
Public Lands and Water Management	10	9	10	0.0	0.0	0.0
Other, Miscellaneous	3,869	3,430	3,529	17.9	15.8	16.4

CNN is fairly similar to the three networks. The most noticeable difference is the category of International Affairs—during the comparable time period, the networks covered that issue area less than in previous decades, while CNN continued to cover it prominently. This may be the case because the networks' news operations cut back budgets for their foreign operations while CNN maintained theirs, probably because CNN has international sister channels.

Public Opinion

Table 2.2 presents the news data for measuring the media's issue agenda. Now, because the theories tested address the relationship between news content and public demands for information, I require a measure of the

Table 2.4. Comparison of Broadcasters to CNN, October 1, 1995–March 31, 2010

Issue	Broadcast (%)	CNN (%)
International Affairs	12.8	28.1
Defense	19.7	19.5
Federal Government Operations	9.0	7.3
Law, Crime	10.9	12.0
Macroeconomics	6.4	1.9
Transportation	4.1	2.4
Health Issues	3.5	1.7
Energy	1.7	0.6
Banking, Finance, and Domestic Commerce	3.5	1.1
Civil Rights	1.8	1.8
Space, Science, Technology, and Communications	1.1	1.1
Labor and Employment	0.8	0.2
Social Welfare	1.8	1.2
Foreign Trade	0.6	0.7
Environment	0.4	0.3
Agriculture	0.4	0.2
Education	0.3	0.1
Community Development and Housing	0.2	0
Public Lands and Water Management	0.0	0
Other, Miscellaneous	21.0	19.6

public's demands for information. For this, I employ a time-series of Gallup's Most Important Problem question (MIP). The MIP asks randomly sampled respondents from the national population to identify the issue that they feel is the most important problem facing the nation. Just like the news issue data in table 2.2, the MIP time-series in table 2.4 is arranged into quarterly averages according to the Baumgartner and Jones coding scheme; this makes for a valid comparison to the news data.[5]

Table 2.5 shows the quarterly mean for each issue area. Macroeconomics is viewed as by far the most important problem, followed by Defense. Transportation and Public Lands & Water Management appear to spark the least public concern. If we compare the MIP data to the news data (in column 3), we see that the issue areas that people most

Table 2.5. Comparison of MIP Data to Broadcast News Data

Issue	Per Quarter Average (percent)	Broadcast (%)
International Affairs	4	12.8
Defense	11	19.7
Federal Government Operations	4	9.0
Law, Crime	10	10.9
Macroeconomics	36	6.4
Transportation	0	4.1
Health Issues	5	3.5
Energy	3	1.7
Banking, Finance, and Domestic Commerce	.2	3.5
Civil Rights	6	1.8
Space, Science, Technology, and Communications	.1	1.1
Labor and Employment	1	0.8
Social Welfare	5	1.8
Foreign Trade	.5	0.6
Environment	1	0.4
Agriculture	.1	0.4
Education	2	0.3
Community Development and Housing	0	0.2
Public Lands and Water Management	0	0.0

often cite as important are also the areas most reported by the networks (I do note that while this relationship is somewhat rough, it has more similarities than differences).

The MIP has been used frequently in the agenda-setting literature and is recognized as the best measure of the public's agenda (Smith 1980; Funkhouser 1973; McCombs and Zhu 1995; Erbring et al. 1980). However, the MIP has its drawbacks (Mackuen and Coombs 1981). First, given that the question asks about the problems facing *this* country, problems in *other* countries will necessarily be overlooked by respondents. While the agenda-setting paradigm would argue that International Affairs should consistently be on the minds of respondents given its prominence in the news, the MIP question is biased against showing this issue on the public agenda. Second, some issues may be salient with the public but not be mentioned by respondents because the question asks respondents to name *problems* rather than issues they deem salient. For example, people may be thinking about the NASA program during historic space launches, but it is unlikely that space exploration will ever register as a high-ranking problem. This highlights a disjuncture between the ideas being tested and the data. In efforts to test how demands for information drive the news issue agenda, it would be most appropriate to have clean measures of both media and public issue salience, but instead, the public opinion data measure salience with a caveat—by asking for "problems." Despite this, important problems facing this country comprise much of the public's issue agenda and probably represent the issues that the public desires information about. Therefore the MIP is the best available indicator of the public's demands for information.

Given that this chapter is interested in the dynamic processes between the media and the public taking place over time, it is appropriate to compare news and public opinion within a time-series format. This is the case because there is a temporal ordering implied in both theories of agenda-setting and audience influence. If agenda-setting occurs, the media report issues first, and then the audience adjusts its assessment of issue salience. If outlets follow audience demands, then the audience will first develop an interest in an issue, with news salience to follow. Thus, we want to grasp the direction of effects to see which occurs first: news content or public issue salience.[6] Knowing this will tell us which conception is in operation.

To identify which comes first, this chapter employs Granger analysis to indicate the direction of statistical causation between news issue coverage and public opinion. This form of analysis is frequently used to study the media-public relationship (e.g. Smith 1987a; Trumbo 1995; Rogers et al. 1991). Essentially, the analysis asks whether variable X "causes" another variable, Y, by incorporating the past history of X into prediction of Y. If the past history of X improves the prediction of Y over the use of Y alone, then X is said to "Granger cause" Y (Granger 1969). In other words, if the audience were to drive news content, then variations in public problem salience would come first and would "Granger-cause" variations in issue coverage. If the media were to drive public salience, then variations in media coverage would come first and would "Granger-cause" variations in public problem salience. Essentially, Granger analysis allows us to answer the question, What drives what?

If we suspect that past values of public concern drove the ebb and flow of news coverage (or vice versa), how far back should we look? One quarter? Two quarters? More? Unfortunately, we have no strong a priori reason to suggest any particular lag. The literature on agenda-setting suggests shorter lags between news content and subsequent public concern, but the findings vary between days, weeks, and months. In addition, there are few guides suggesting an exact time lapse between a change in public opinion and the change in news content that might presumably follow.

At best, we can deduce that regardless of the causal direction, a lag of less than four quarters is appropriate. We would not expect public opinion from more than nine months ago to affect current news. If reporters were to follow public opinion in constructing news content, it might take some time for reporters to become conscious of changing opinion, and then implement changes in reporting to follow. But, we would expect reporters to adjust their reporting to follow opinion that is reasonably recent. Therefore, I test the relationships between public issue salience and issue coverage at one, two, and three lags. I report a summary of these results and note when the results are not consistent across lag specification.

With this said, these expectations will be mediated by the amount of public concern and news attention for each issue area. For example, some issues will never garner much public concern or appreciable news coverage. With these issues, I expect to find no relationship. And, we may see bidirectional relationships exhibited by some issue areas because public concern drives news firms while at the same time, news firms react to public concern.

Table 2.6 summarizes the findings.[7] First, many issues show evidence of audience influence over content: the ebb and flow of public concern comes first and drives the media's coverage of these issues. This is the case with stories addressing Civil Rights, Defense, Foreign Trade, Macroeconomics, Health, Law & Crime, and Federal Government Operations. As public concern over these issues increases, the broadcasters follow by reporting more stories about them. Take the Watergate scandal, which drove much Federal Government Operations coverage in the

Table 2.6. Summary Results of Granger Causality Tests

Audience-Driven	Agenda-Setting	No Relationship
Civil Rights[a]	Civil Rights[b]	Agriculture
Defense	Law and Crime	Banking/Finance/Commerce
Foreign Trade[d]	Energy	Community Development
Macroeconomics	Social Welfare[c]	Education
Health[a]		Environment
Law and Crime		International Affairs
Federal Government Operations		Labor
		Public Lands/Water
		Space/Science/Technology
		Transportation

[a] Relationship significant only at one lag.
[b] Relationship significant only at two and three lags.
[c] Relationship significant at two lags.
[d] Relationship significant at one and three lags.

early 1970s. The story broke in the nightly news, and hit a lull for some time—probably because the story was not that interesting or palatable for audiences in the early going. But as audiences became more interested in Nixon's transgressions, the broadcasters increased their coverage until the story dominated the nightly news. Or, stepping outside of the data for a moment, consider coverage of the War on Terror from 2001 through 2013. The wars in Iraq and Afghanistan were highly salient in the news through 2008, but as the economy worsened and became more salient, the news followed. Even though the wars were still in full swing as President Obama entered office, coverage of Defense issues dipped.

That seven broad issue areas are driven by audience concerns speaks to the pervasiveness of audience influence. Traditional models of journalism would suggest that journalists should not be constrained or influenced by the public in this way. Journalists should report issues because the journalists themselves see value in the stories for society. If journalists instead put their thumbs to the wind to see what audiences want to hear about, then there is little guarantee that the issues then reported would meet the broader interests of democratic society.

The issue of Civil Rights shows evidence of a bidirectional relationship. News drives public-problem salience while at the same time problem salience drives news content. This is an issue that has come in and out of the public interest during the last five decades, and has had varying numbers of large-scale events to report on. Besides Civil Rights, four other issues show evidence of agenda-setting. News coverage of Law & Crime, Energy, and Social Welfare appears to drive the public's concern for those issues. It may be that the media are covering events that the audience is not initially concerned about. For example, the reporting of crime often does not coincide with crime rates or, in this case, concern over crime. News firms may report on the issue because the issue area encompasses events that are violent and fantastic, and on their own can draw in audiences regardless of a demand for information.

A series of issues shows no relationship between public concern and news coverage during the entirety of the time frame investigated.

In these issues, public concern barely registers, and as a result, news firms see no demand. These issues are Agriculture, Banking, Community Development, Education, Health, International Affairs, Labor, Public Lands and Water, Space and Technology, and Transportation. All of these issues are on average mentioned by 5 percent or less as the most important problem facing the country; some are mentioned less than 1 percent on average. Also, coverage of these issues, with the exception of International Affairs, is sporadic and infrequent. One example of this is the issue of Agriculture. Stories about agriculture comprised half of 1 percent of the news data, and only an average of a tenth of a percent of the public identified the issue as the most important problem. This suggests that the lack of public concern over these issues, combined with few newsworthy events, leads the networks to ignore them.

The import of the above findings is that when using methods designed to more fairly test audience influence versus agenda-setting, we find results showing that yes, indeed, the audience does appear to influence the media—even traditional outlets such as the nightly network news programs. Granger tests do have inherent limitations—they exclude other variables that may be involved in the audience-media relationship, they don't show true causality, and they make no claim as to why one variable might precede another. For this reason, the Granger results should be viewed more as strongly suggestive than as inherently indicative (I do note that more complicated tests show support for the results here). In addition, there does not seem to be a clear rule as to why some issues will exhibit one relationship and other issues will exhibit the opposite. This deserves further study—but for present purposes, it is more important to note that the audience appears to exert a good deal of influence over the news agenda. Finally, this chapter examines the nightly network news programs. We can make some generalizations to other forms of news, but we should be cautious. On one hand, we do know that studies have found evidence of audience influence in newspapers and other forms of news in the past—and currently, internet sources of news use measures, such as the number of clicks or comments a story receives, to formulate future reporting. On the other hand, audience influence may rear its head in different ways at different outlets and mediums, and during different time periods.

Conclusion

Agenda-setting studies led to a paradigm shift in the way scholars view the influence of news over the masses. On one hand, hundreds of extant studies show that the news has the ability to influence the public's assessment of issue salience. This effect is not in doubt. When audiences do not know about an important event, the media can inform them and increase the salience of it. On the other hand, extant studies also show that news firms follow audience concerns in choosing which stories to report as well. Given these disparate sets of findings, researchers have long struggled to understand the circumstances under which the audience would influence news coverage. This chapter's results suggest that the audience has a stronger influence over news content than many have previously thought—these findings are probably due to the use of broad issue areas, a long time frame, and larger units of time.

When they follow audience demands, reporters have less room to exhibit independent judgment. For example, stories about public education may offer the audience little in the way of excitement, but the public education system may be in serious need of reform. Should journalists ignore this problem until the public begins to exhibit a demand for coverage of public education? Traditional models of journalism would suggest *no*. Conversely, should news outlets bombard audiences with particular stories simply because they offer excitement and intrigue? The answer is still probably *no*. In the last two decades, news outlets dedicated a great deal of precious news space to coverage of celebrity trials such as the O. J. Simpson murder trial and the Michael Jackson child molestation trial. While the events that precipitated these trials were tragic, this coverage was merely designed to draw audiences. Theories of traditional journalism would probably argue that the media blitzes surrounding these entertaining events had little to do with the best interests of the public.

This chapter suggests that audiences have a great deal of influence over the news. This finding goes a long way towards explaining why the news is what it is. Audiences demand certain sets of information, and the news responds because it has financial incentives to do so. This explanation of news content differs greatly from explanations grounded in traditional journalism.

Chapter 3 builds on the framework presented here by incorporating audience demands for political gratification. In addition, the analysis in chapter 3 will include a variety of control variables measuring the actions of government and objective events and conditions. The analysis in chapter 3, despite the inclusion of these additional factors, will not only provide support for the framework in this chapter but also demonstrate that mass ideological and partisan preferences also appear to strongly predict the issues covered in the nightly news.

3

Demands for Gratification

Competing in the National News Economy

You have to pound home a strong point of view. If you're
not . . . people won't listen, or watch.
—Bill O'Reilly, May 8, 2002

Currently the host of the number one cable news program in the United
States, *The O'Reilly Factor*, Bill O'Reilly is perhaps the poster child for
having a strong point of view. He is a hero to many conservatives, but
lambasted by many on the Left. O'Reilly's career caricatures the recent
history of the news industry—he started off as a broadcast journalist for
local and national news outlets, and then became more tabloid-ish as the
host of *Inside Edition*. In the mid-1990s he moved into more ideologically driven news with the emergence of the Fox News Channel. He has
since had the highest ratings in cable news for more than a decade, and
in addition had a brief but successful stint on talk radio.

While trained as a journalist, O'Reilly is quick to admit that his
popular cable show is not journalism in the traditional sense—instead
he refers to most of his work as "analysis." But whether we consider
The O'Reilly Factor to be traditional news or something else, it is the

highest-rated cable news show. People turn to O'Reilly for, at least what they consider to be, *news*. As the above quotation suggests, much of the news business is driven by points of view. Sometimes these points of view are more overt, as with the Fox News Channel or MSNBC; at other times these points of view are more opaque, as with the broadcast networks. In either case, news outlets must have a point of view that draws in audiences large enough to attract advertisers and revenues. Given audiences' natural desire to hear news that shares their own points of view, successful news outlets do their best to match their programming to the point of view of as much of the audience as possible. This chapter shows how both traditional outlets and the newer cable outlets have attempted to follow audiences' points of view in constructing the news.

Using data from the nightly network news, the preceding chapter demonstrated how demands for information led to the reporting of particular issue areas. Two broad points arise from chapter 2. First, news programs can focus public attention on certain issues—this is agenda-setting. But, this effect is limited because news firms often report on issue areas that are already viewed as important by the public. This leaves news programming with little room to affect the audience's assessment of issue salience. Second, because news outlets appear to provide news in response to the audience's demands for information, they may be engaging in *civic-minded journalism* because news firms provide information demanded by citizens. On one hand, this may be good—if audiences can identify issues that need attention and resolution, then news firms should respond. On the other hand, this form of journalism may simply indicate evidence of profit seeking. Regardless, news firms are following audience demands whether they are being civic minded or simply responding to markets and chasing audience size.

This chapter more closely examines the motivations of news firms to shape content, this time from the perspective of demands for gratification. To examine how the audience's desire for gratification affects news, I begin with a case study tracking the development of the three major cable news networks, CNN, FNC, and MSNBC. These three networks provide an ideal case study because, unlike the three broadcast network news programs, these networks have used their content most blatantly to chase after different portions of ideologically segmented audiences. Because of the nature of 24-hour news and the economics of cable, cable news providers are able to position themselves along an ideological continuum, having only to appeal to a segment of the broader audience. Not only do demands for ideologically gratifying news drive specific content on each channel, but the distribution of ideology in the public has driven the entire structure of the cable news market.

Following this case study, the analysis returns to the nightly news data introduced in chapter 2 tracking issue coverage. However, instead of focusing on how the broadcast firms interact with demands for information over time, the analysis explores another opinion that firms may seek to gratify, partisanship. The analysis will show how broadcasters alter their substantive issue coverage over time to follow changing levels of partisanship in the mass public. With the two analyses, this chapter will not only demonstrate how news firms cater to audience demands for gratification, but it will also provide leverage on determining the reasons why news firms follow audience opinions in some instances.

This chapter proceeds as follows: I begin by examining demands for gratification and why the audience prefers news that agrees with their predispositions. I then detail the development of the cable news market and argue that it has been driven by the ideological demands of audiences, rather than by the ideologies of the owners or journalists. Finally, I examine how the audience's partisanship drives even the more traditional broadcast firms to alter their substantive issue coverage to gratify audiences. I conclude this chapter by discussing how journalistic independence is constrained by audiences' demands for gratifying news, and how this in turn hurts news quality and audiences.

Demands for Gratification

In chapter 1, I argued that on one hand, traditional conceptions of journalism should drive journalists to ignore audience demands when choosing what stories to report. On the other hand, news firms have financial incentives to follow demands in shaping news content. U.S. news firms exist in a capitalist system and therefore rely on revenue (from either advertisers or audiences) to stay in business. In short, news firms need audiences. When they lose audience size, they lose revenue. When revenue drops below a critical mass, the outlet goes out of business.

To stay in business, firms attempt to draw in audiences by meeting three major types of demand: for entertainment, for information, and for gratification. When meeting demands for entertainment, firms may report violent, sensational, or otherwise eye-catching stories. Firms may also highlight human-interest stories to entertain audiences (e.g. "Dog Calls 911 to Save Owner"). When meeting demands for information, firms may follow audience concerns and report stories containing information addressing those specific concerns. If audiences became concerned with the amount or adequacy of social welfare spending in this country, then firms might begin reporting stories about Social Security, national health care reform, and food stamps. However, when firms meet demands for gratification, they will report stories that make audiences "feel good" about their previously held beliefs. Following demands for gratification does not provide a traditional conception of journalism—the topics, guests, opinions, and analyses are chosen specifically to appeal to the previously held beliefs of the audiences. Such news does not challenge audience beliefs, provide new perspectives, or aim to present "truth." This essentially creates an ideological "echo chamber" for viewers, who will not be exposed to news that challenges their belief systems. To use a well-worn aphorism, people are inclined to use information the way a drunk might use a lamppost—for support rather than for illumination.

Psychologists have long shown that people are resistant to messages that challenge their ideological beliefs: people tend to challenge information discordant with their previous beliefs more than information with which they a priori agree (Lord et al. 1979). For example, if a die-hard Obama supporter were presented with evidence detailing how Obama's policies have damaged the economy, it is likely that that person would consider that evidence highly suspect, or accept the information but claim it doesn't matter anyway. This psychological resistance translates into preferences for news: people prefer news that supports their beliefs and avoid news that does not (Iyengar and Hahn 2009; Iyengar et al. 2008). Because general news content is inherently political, this chapter focuses on political belief systems, such as ideology and partisanship, and how those affect news content. These preferences create powerful incentives for news firms, and invariably lead them to alter their substantive news coverage in a way that deviates from what we would expect if traditional journalistic norms were followed (Endersby and Ognianova 1997). This takes place in one form or another, and in some degree, in all outlets, but it is most visibly the case in cable news. Since cable news providers do not compete on the price they charge consumers, they compete with each other by differentiating their programming; this gives audiences choices for best meeting their demands (e.g. Bae 1999).

Generally, it is very difficult to show that news firms follow audience demands. Unlike veteran newsman Ted Koppell, whose concerns about news firms opened this book, news outlets rarely admit to following public demands in designing their content. Furthermore, journalists, editors, and producers who do follow audience demands do not even need to know that they are doing so. The incentives for them are clear and continually reinforced. News providers simply need to follow their economic incentives to be successful; they never need to be conscious of it. In this sense, understanding the effect of markets on news outlets takes on the appearance of a structural argument: the broader system of incentives drives the micro-behaviors of individual actors without them ever having to know or acknowledge it. Of course, while they do not have to be aware, they often are, and often pursue purposeful strategies of following audience tastes.

So how can we better understand the forces that drive decisions about news content? One solution would be to interview journalists, editors, producers, and managers and simply ask them. Unfortunately, it is unlikely that news firms would admit that concerns about audience size drive their reporting. In fact, most news outlets market themselves as doing the exact opposite. Outlets use catch phrases such as "the news you need to know" or "keeping you up to date on the important issues." News firms do not overtly market their products as "the most entertaining," "news that makes you feel good about yourself," or "news that can capture a large audience." In designing content to draw in large audiences, news firms do not want to alert those large audiences to their incentive structures. And furthermore, news managers may feel that publicly acknowledging the idea of chasing demand would be bad for newsroom morale (Underwood 1993). This allows both audiences and news firms to coexist in a mutual state of denial. Audiences can deny that they watch news to be entertained or otherwise gratified (they may not consciously know it, anyway), and news outlets can deny that they construct news simply for monetary purposes. In short, evidence for profit seeking on the part of news firms will be hard to come by simply by asking news personnel about their incentives. Another way we can assess the impact of demands for gratification is by comparing the audience's political opinions to news content; this can indicate whether news firms follow audience opinions in order to provide them with gratification.

This chapter is designed not only to show how audiences affect news firms but also to show that news firms are engaging in profit seeking by following audience demands for gratification. In chapter 2, I operationalized demands for information using the Most Important Problem question. Over time, the concerns expressed by the public varied—at some points, the public was most concerned with Economics; at other points in time the public was most concerned with other issues. Demands for entertainment are more difficult to measure, and it is unclear whether the level of demand for entertainment changes over time. However, demands for gratification, if we view them as stemming from political opinions, do change over time because political opinions at the mass level change over time. We know this because surveys have measured many political opinions for a sufficient period of time to observe over-time variation.

This chapter measures demands for gratification as mass ideology and mass partisanship. If these opinions were to predict the distribution of the news market, or subsequent substantive coverage, this would then probably indicate that news firms followed demands for gratification. Such a finding would indicate that journalists were not engaging in traditional journalistic practices because they were following mass public opinion (whether they were consciously aware of it, or admit it, or not).

Ideology and Partisanship

There are many audience opinions or preferences that news firms may account for. For several vital reasons, this chapter focuses on ideology and partisanship. To be clear on definitions, "ideology" is a person's core political values that structure other political opinions, and "partisanship" is a preference for one political party, usually Republican or Democrat, over the other (Erikson and Tedin 2005:66, 77).

First, ideology and partisanship are perhaps the most important and influential political opinions in the United States. Beginning in the early half of last century, political scientists began conceptualizing ideology and partisanship as deeply held opinions stemming from long-engrained psychological processes (Campbell et al. 1960; Campbell et al. 1954; Campbell et al. 1966; Key 1955). In this, citizens were socialized into having an ideology and partisan attachment; these socializing forces came from family, education, friends and acquaintances, occupation, racial and ethnic ties, socioeconomic status, culture, and religion. As people grow older, their ideologies and partisan attachments take hold and generally remain stable throughout their lifetimes. For example, a person who identifies as a Democrat today will probably be a Democrat fifty years from now. People overwhelmingly tend to vote in line with their partisanship and ideology, and their other more specific opinions are formed as a consequence of those larger opinions. Accordingly, ideology and partisanship are perhaps the most important political opinions that one can hold. If one were to seek gratification for one's politics, one would want coverage that coincided with these two opinions. In this regard, then, ideology and partisanship provide excellent indicators of demands for gratification.

But, while partisanship and ideology are highly stable on the micro-level, they are somewhat volatile on the macro-level (MacKuen et al. 1989; Box-Steffensmeier and DeBoef 2001). We can measure variation in ideology and partisanship, and it is this variation that national news firms will chase over time. Some reasons for over-time variation exist on the micro-level. First, some people do adjust their ideology or party identification over time. People may claim less of an allegiance to a party if it has performed poorly in recent years, or if they have little confidence in that party's leaders (Fiorina 1981; Erikson et al. 1998). Then there is generational turnover—as newer generations come and older generations go, the make-up of mass opinion will change (Abramson 1976; Craig and Bennett 1997). But, regardless of the cause, mass opinions vary over time, and if firms follow these opinions, then we should observe over-time variation in news.

Second, this chapter focuses on partisanship and ideology because studies showing the stability of these opinions at the *micro-level* suggest that, because of this stability, these opinions are not affected by news coverage (Hopkins and Ladd 2012). This is very important—in attempting to understand the relationship between news coverage and public opinions, scholars want to be very careful that they are correctly specifying the direction of influence between the two (this was the focus of chapter 2). Simply showing that opinions and issue coverage are correlated might indicate that opinions cause news coverage, or it might indicate the exact opposite. By using ideology and partisanship as an indicator of audience demands for gratification, this analysis can be more certain that any correlations found between these and news coverage are not indicative of news coverage causing ideology or partisanship to fluctuate. (To err on the safe side, the latter half of this chapter employs statistical techniques to account for the possibility of bidirectional effects, and I find none.)

Third, ideology and partisanship are particularly appealing opinions for this study because traditional conceptions of journalism do *not* lead us to expect that changes in these opinions should lead to altered reporting. In fact, professional norms of journalism lead us to expect that news people report issues *independently* of these audience opinions. There is simply little room within the rubric of traditional journalism for reporters to follow ideology and partisanship when crafting news coverage. Further, if news firms followed changes in these opinions, it would probably indicate profit-driven reporting rather than civic-minded journalism because reporters would not be meeting needs for vital information—they would instead be attempting to gratify preexisting opinions.

Finally, news firms have access to measures of the distribution of ideology and partisanship in the population. Polls measuring these attitudes are readily available to all news organizations; these polls are taken regularly and their results are often reported as news stories in and of themselves. Therefore, news firms not only have access to the necessary information to account for mass partisanship when allocating issue coverage, but their reporting suggests that they are consciously aware of its fluctuations as well.

This chapter now provides a case study examining how the distribution of political ideology in the audience has shaped the branding of the entire cable news market. The history of cable news networks will show how they branded themselves to follow market demands, and how their choices of which segments of the market to cater to have largely determined their success in terms of audience size. Following that, the analysis will return to the nightly broadcast news networks. A statistical analysis will argue that even the broadcasters, who are supposedly more "traditional" than their cable counterparts (Entman 2005), follow changes in the mass distribution of partisan attachments in the audience by adjusting their reporting on certain substantive issue areas over time.

Ideology and Cable News

The delivery of news has changed greatly in the last thirty years; these changes have come to a point where, for many people, the days of having only three major channels are almost unimaginable (Tewksbury and Rittenberg 2012:1). In fact, the majority of the people reading this book will have been born years if not decades after cable went into widespread use. Many of the changes that have occurred have been due to emerging technologies that made the delivery of news and other programming relatively inexpensive compared to older modes of delivery. This is especially true in terms of delivering news to audiences outside of urban areas—cable came about because of the difficulty broadcast signals had reaching mountainous and rural areas. The broadcasters concentrated their signals in the populated areas, so alternative means were necessary to deliver television signals to less populated areas.

In the 1940s and 1950s, cable providers simply provided the means for broadcast channels to reach remote audiences with their programming. However, in the late 1950s, cable providers began to provide their own programming to compete with the broadcasters. Broadcasters, fearing a loss of viewership due to the emergence of competition on cable, began lobbying Congress and the Federal Communications Commission to more tightly regulate cable. The broadcasters' argument was that increased competition would lower advertising revenue, and therefore decrease the quality of programming that broadcasters could provide. In short, the broadcasters wanted the government to help them keep their monopoly. While the FCC was at first reluctant, claiming that cable was out of their purview, they eventually regulated cable nearly to the point that it became unviable. This ended in the 1970s when the courts began to overturn many of the FCC regulations. With the loosening of regulations, cable programming immediately began to thrive and expand. In the 1970s there were about twenty-five cable channels, and by 1990 this had nearly tripled (Hillstorm 2006). Now, audiences choose among hundreds of channels.

Before the prominence of cable television, many, particularly on the Right, suspected that the broadcast news shows were liberally biased. Despite an outward appearance of adherence to traditional journalistic standards, the networks' coverage of some stories, such as those having to do with the Vietnam War, led many to believe that the networks were pushing a liberal point of view. The notion of liberal bias was sometimes used as a galvanizing rally cry for leaders on the Right; for example, in the late 1960s Vice-President Spiro Agnew referred to reporters as "nattering nabobs of negativism." While systematic evidence of liberal bias by the networks during the pre-cable time frame was wanting (Russo 1971–1972), the idea of a liberal bias took hold. As more sophisticated methods of measuring bias became available, it became fairly clear that not only were the network reporters aligned mostly on the Left (Lichter et al. 1986), but that coverage tilted left as well (Groseclose and Milyo 2005).

Given that there were three networks, one might have expected them either to position their content to the ideological median (where the vast majority of the population is) or to segment the audience along ideological lines by moving to the left or the right. Instead, the three networks, by most accounts, showed a leftward tilt, but stayed close enough to the ideological median so as not to overtly alienate rightward-leaning audiences (D'Alessio and Allen 2000). Many describe this leftward tilt as driven by the ideologies of the network newspeople (Goldberg 2002). This behavior appears to be in line with some economic models of media behavior, which suggest that liberal reporters will be able to affect coverage at the edges, so long as viewership is not significantly damaged by it (Bovitz et al. 2002; Sutter 2001). In the case of the broadcasters, they had a near-monopoly and could get away with leftward tilt (it remains curious, however, that none of the three networks ever defected and positioned themselves more distinctly).

As a consequence of the government's deregulation of cable, the all-news network CNN was introduced in 1980. CNN was a response to the increased number of cable systems and subscribers, as well as to the demand for more news programming. CNN's 24-hour format on the one hand gave audiences news at any time of the day; on the other hand, the network had to fill twenty-four hours with news. Up until that point, the evening national news programs had only occupied a half-hour a day. To accommodate the 24-hour schedule, CNN filled its programming with shows focusing on specific topics. *Moneyline* (eventually *Lou Dobbs Tonight*), hosted by Lou Dobbs, focused on financial stories. *Crossfire*, originally hosted by Pat Buchanan and Tom Braden, focused on hot-button national political issues. In order to accommodate those who simply wanted the headlines without the other more nuanced news programming, and also to stave off emerging competition, CNN spun off a second network, CNN2, which later became Headline News (HLN).

CNN, given its 24-hour nature, was different from the network news-casts in many respects. But, it also captured and repackaged some of what the networks had been doing for some time, but in a longer format. For example, CNN hard news programs were not unlike the network news shows, and many of the other shows on CNN were not a far cry from the broadcast networks' news magazines such as *20/20* and *60 Minutes*. Like the broadcasters, CNN gained a reputation for mainstream news that had a liberal tilt to it (Turner 2007). Anecdotal evidence frequently surfaced to support the claims of liberal bias. For example, the conservative Media Research Center found that the broadcast networks and CNN covered issues differently depending on the party of the president—when Republican George H. W. Bush was president, there were seventy-one stories about the homeless on the broadcasts and CNN evening newscasts. But, when Democrat Bill Clinton was in the White House, there were only nine (Goldberg 2002:79). While coverage of homelessness went down 87 percent, actual homelessness did not face any such sharp decline.

In the mid-1990s, CNN faced legitimate competition, both from news magnate Rupert Murdoch and from NBC and Microsoft Corporation. Given the increasing reach of cable into U.S. homes, and the decreasing production costs of starting a cable network, Murdoch's Fox News Channel and MSNBC (a creation of Microsoft and NBC) entered the cable news market in 1996. Part of the reason for their emergence was a market demand for higher-quality news programming with a higher quantity of news stories. CNN at the time had a near monopoly in the cable news market, and to many, the quality of the programming had dipped as a result. For example, on entering the cable market, Murdoch said. "To be a meaningful broadcaster, you have to have news. . . . [I]t will be much better than CNN. . . . I watch CNN on TV, but it doesn't have much news. . . . I watch it when I get on my exercise machine in the morning. There are long commercial breaks and it's quite repetitive." Responding to CNN's programming, both FNC and MSNBC adopted an alternative style to CNN, bringing more entertaining hosts and guests, and offering a less "traditional" and more opinionated style (Ladd 2012:68).

But for FNC, the motivation was not simply to provide higher-quality news with fewer commercial breaks than CNN; it was instead to fill the needs of an underserved market. Murdoch, like a large portion of the American public, saw CNN and the other existing news choices as too liberal. Murdoch believed that those audiences who viewed CNN and other news outlets as too liberal would prefer an outlet reporting news that was less liberal, and perhaps even overtly conservative. He thought that not only could he steal conservative audiences from existing news sources but also he could increase the overall size of the market by bringing in audiences who were currently disaffected. FNC took a long-time complaint against the media and cast it as a problem of ideological positioning: since many audiences viewed CNN as liberal, that indicated that those audiences were more conservative than CNN's coverage. Accordingly, those audiences could be lured away with news that more closely matched their ideological predispositions. The recipe for FNC was to cater to the demands of the underserved right-of-left-of-center market. Of course, Murdoch publicly denied that his intent was to provide a conservative alternative per se, but rather claimed that he wanted to bring "balance" to television journalism (Collins 2004:24).

Murdoch's first step was to bring in Roger Ailes, a well-known Republican strategist, to handle the day-to-day operations of the network. Ailes's initial strategy appeared to be three-pronged. First, he attempted to move the very popular conservative talk radio format onto television (Brock and Rabin-Hayt 2012:16). This involved bringing in talk radio hosts such as Sean Hannity and, later, Glen Beck and Laura Ingraham. Second, Ailes attempted to draw a distinction between Fox and the other stations through marketing taglines and content. Fox was marketed as "Fair and Balanced," a line subtly hinting that the competition was neither fair nor balanced, and indeed was liberally biased. Third, Fox's content provided conservative points of view, conservative leaders and issues, and a sometimes antagonistic view of the Left. Central to Fox's programming has been the cultivation of conservative hosts and commentators such as Bill O'Reilly, Karl Rove, and Charles Krauthammer. As media scholar Alison Dagnes (2010:81) puts it, this strategy created an audience that Fox News continues to cater to.

> Once Fox News Channel gained a significant conservative audience with its personality-driven pundit programming, the rest of Fox News programming followed suit to create the brand we see today. By asserting a liberal bias in the rest of the mainstream media, Fox News has carved for itself a niche audience of conservative viewers. It is in Fox's best interest to maintain this audience through consistently conservative programming.

Fox's strategies to pull in audiences by all accounts worked. As media critics David Brock and Ari Rabin-Hayt commented (2012:16), "[T]his model was successful at the tail end of the Clinton administration and was even better suited to cheerlead for George W. Bush. In less than a decade, Fox News president Roger Ailes created for Rupert Murdoch a network with a built-in audience driven by its conservative ideology." Ratings soared in comparison to competitors. For example, in the early 2000s, only FNC saw a growth in viewership, mainly from a growing conservative viewership, while other news outlets either flat-lined or saw their audience shares decline (Selepak 2006). During the 2000 Florida recount, conservatives turned to Fox as the place to get news, and as a consequence, it passed MSNBC in the ratings, averaging more than one million viewers per night in November 2000 (Brock and Rabin-Hayt 2012:53). Going toward the middle of the decade, the percentage of people watching Fox rose to 25 percent in 2004, giving the Fox News Channel a larger audience than CNN and becoming Republicans' most credible source for the news among television and cable news outlets (Selepak 2006). This trend continues, with Fox consistently achieving starkly higher ratings than their competitors in 2012. But on the other end of the sword, FNC's branding has made it less credible with those on the Left and their least trusted news source among television and cable news outlets (Selepak 2006).

It is true that Murdoch and Roger Ailes are both political conservatives. Even though Murdoch said in several interviews that he was responding to a market demand for less liberal news, there are many who contend that the personal views of Murdoch and Ailes drive their programming, perhaps for purposes of propaganda (i.e. Franken 2003; Alterman 2003). But, even if these contentions were true—that somehow Murdoch and Ailes were involved in a conspiracy to mislead and misinform voters for their personal political agendas—it would not diminish the influence of audiences. Murdoch and Ailes did not succeed because they produced news that accorded with *their* views, but because they produced news that accorded with the views of a large underserved portion of the market. If audiences chose not to watch FNC, then it would suffer the lower ratings of its competitors (and perhaps have to reorganize or go out of business). While arguments persist that FNC's conservative programming comes from its ownership and management, one need not look further than the audience to understand Fox News programming. It is difficult to levy a charge of propaganda if the audience self-selects. But if one were still not convinced that audiences drive FNC, then the histories of MSNBC and CNN may shed further light.

MSNBC, like Fox, arose in the mid-1990s as a response to CNN's monopoly over cable news. The original strategy was simply one of quality: MSNBC wanted to show more news than CNN, with perhaps more in-depth issue coverage. MSNBC's brand was therefore somewhat undefined during its first decade, as "the channel bounced from one programming idea to another" (Shelter 2010). As Salon.com reported of MSNBC's early years (Kornacki 2011),

> For the first decade or so of its existence, the cable news channel had only the vaguest of identities. Every few months, a new host or two would be tossed into the lineup, only to be shuffled around a few months later, and put out to pasture a few months after that. One day, [liberal] Phil Donahue was the network's prime-time face; the next it was [conservative]

Alan Keyes. Sometimes it seemed like the only programming MSNBC actually believed in was Don Imus's tired minstrel show in the mornings and weird prison documentaries on the weekends.

MSNBC's strategy during those years was not to chase an ideological segment of the audience (like FNC), but rather to provide programming that as a whole would appeal to the entirety of the potential audience. During the mid-2000s the channel attempted to compete for Bill O'Reilly's audience with the program *Scarborough Country*, hosted by former Republican congressman Joe Scarborough. The show featured a similar format, but was only able to garner a small audience of about three hundred thousand per night. The channel brought in libertarian Tucker Carlson to host his own show after his departure from CNN's *Crossfire*, and paired him with the progressive Rachel Maddow. That show only lasted three years. MSNBC's biggest problem was that it could not compete for conservative viewers against Fox, who had cornered that market. This left them to compete with CNN for the remainder of the cable news audience. As a result, both MSNBC's and CNN's ratings were poor.

However, fortunes changed for MSNBC for two reasons. First, public skepticism of the Iraq War grew during George W. Bush's second term. This provided an issue that MSNBC could brand itself on (Sherman 2010). The turning point came in the summer of 2006 (Kornacki 2011):

At the end of his Aug. 30, 2006 show, Olbermann looked directly into the camera and spoke: "The man who sees absolutes where all other men see nuances and shades of meaning is either a prophet or a quack. Donald H. Rumsfeld is not a prophet." His blistering takedown of the defense secretary was a viral sensation. Millions of liberals were equally exasperated with the Bush administration; but few could express themselves as exquisitely and powerfully as Olbermann. They asked for more, and Olbermann gladly gave it to them; over the next few years, there would be dozens of "special comments," each delivered in the same dramatic style. . . . He became an all-purpose critic of the administration and its cheerleaders, and then of the Republican Party and the modern brand of conservatism it has embraced. For years, liberals had watched the growth of Fox News with dismay and alarm. With "Countdown," they finally had their own prime-time cable news show to flock to. Olbermann embraced the rivalry, skewering Fox and its personalities—particularly Bill O'Reilly—with biting humor and sarcasm, daring them to respond and acknowledge him. His ratings climbed—not to Fox levels, to be sure, but to levels that had been unheard of at MSNBC.

This showed the leadership at MSNBC that there was a market to be served, but in this case, a liberal market.

Then in 2008, with new leadership at the helm (Phil Griffin was named president), MSNBC began to rebrand itself as a liberally minded network that could speak to those disaffected during the George W. Bush years. It helped that a presidential election campaign was underway with a media sensation, Barack Obama, as the Democratic nominee. As *New York Magazine* (Sherman 2010) reported of MSNBC's move into second place ahead of CNN,

> "Fox figured it out that you have to stand for something in cable," MSNBC president Phil Griffin says. Since Griffin was appointed in 2008, the network has adopted much of the Fox News playbook. "What we're doing is targeting an audience," Griffin says. "In television, and in particular cable television, brand is everything," NBC Universal CEO Jeff Zucker told me, before he announced his departure two weeks ago. "For a long time, MSNBC floundered with its identity." . . . While Zucker and Griffin are both liberals, they got in the politics business for the ratings, and MSN-BC's new identity has been a ratings boon. . . . Griffin, now that he's found ratings religion, is doubling down. In April 2009, he hired the liberal radio host Ed Schultz for a 6 p.m. show. This past summer, MSNBC announced it was developing a 10 p.m. show for Lawrence O'Donnell to replace reruns of Olbermann. Recently, MSNBC tried to buy the Huffington Post (Huffington Post founder Ken Lerer rejected the offer). The network hired Spike Lee to shoot a multi-million-dollar advertising campaign and developed

its own obtuse slogan: "Lean Forward." The tagline "defines us and defines our competition," said Phil Griffin, the president of MSNBC. . . . "When you're clear about who you are, you actually make money," said Sharon Otterman, the chief marketing officer for MSNBC.

Following Olbermann's success, MSNBC engaged in a series of on-air personnel changes. Don Imus was let go due to racially insensitive remarks he made on air. Conservatives Tucker Carlson's and Joe Scarborough's shows were canceled; Carlson eventually moved to Fox News, and Scarborough moved into the then-empty morning spot on MSNBC. Liberals Rachel Maddow, Al Sharpton, and Ed Schultz were given hour-long shows in the primetime line-up. And more recently, Pat Buchanan, the only prominent conservative commentator left, was let go due to passages in his book *Suicide of a Superpower: Will America Survive to 2025?* which enflamed liberal sensibilities. These changes solidified MSNBC as the bastion of liberal and progressive thought. It was unlikely that MSNBC would overcome FNC's ratings because of ideological marketing: conservatives outnumber liberals in the United States in polls, often two to one (Mak 2012). This just about explains Fox's ratings advantage over MSNBC. But, the moves MSNBC made brought them out of the doldrums and into second place.

The case of MSNBC shows the power of the audience to affect programming. MSNBC began to capitalize on public sentiment, first with Olbermann's critiques of the war, and then with a new evening line-up and branding strategy. Those in charge of MSNBC are no doubt liberal; and many of the liberal on-air personalities are probably sincere, perhaps to the point of zealotry. But, they always were—even before the network began to "Lean Forward." Therefore, the changes in political branding at MSNBC would be tough to pin on the ideologies of the management.

CNN, due to both FNC's and MSNBC's cornering of the ideological extremities, has been the biggest loser since the market expansion in 1996 (Joyella 2010).

When year-end figures are released soon, it's almost certain to be CNN's worst performance in over a decade. According to Nielsen Media

Research, for the year to date CNN's ratings among viewers 25–54 (the key news demographic) cratered in 2010, plummeting 34 percent in primetime—the biggest decline of any network. Fox News, by comparison, was off 7 percent compared to 2009, but still easily dominated primetime with an average of 503,000 viewers 25–54. MSNBC (off 10 percent) came in second with 249,000. CNN was third with 174,000 followed closely by sister network HLN with 144,000 (another big drop—viewership off 32 percent from 2009).

By not overtly branding itself as FNC and MSNBC had, CNN fumbled terribly; it went from a powerhouse monopoly to third place. CNN continues to offer competitive, high-quality programming; however, the supposedly ideologically neutral programming does not have the appeal that the more ideologically branded news has. Those who watch television news in the current market choose to do so over hundreds of other channels—this indicates that those audiences have a strong interest in politics and current events. This interest often correlates with a well-defined ideology on the right or left.

In response to their steady slide, CNN attempted to shift its programming to attract what it now considers to be the underserved audience: racial minorities. Given that minorities are less likely to be conservative than whites, and that the progressive movement is also predominantly white, CNN has seen an opening to target its programming to blacks and Hispanics, who may not be quite as attracted to either FNC or MSNBC. CNN had attracted a racially diverse group of on-air personalities, including Rick Sanchez, Soledad O'Brien, Fredricka Whitfield, and Don Lemmon. During the election campaign of 2008, CNN performed well with the minority audience, but lost ground shortly thereafter. CNN has since targeted its on-air talent and content toward luring back racial minorities. For example,

Mark Nelson, vice president and senior executive producer at CNN Productions, is interested in bridging that gap. "We are what we air, and we air what we are," he says, explaining his network's Diversity Initiative, which was conceived by Jim Walton, president of CNN Worldwide. "It's a diversity of ideas, diversity of people, diversity of experiences . . . diversity on our air." In keeping with this vision, CNN will premiere *Black in America 2*, the follow-up to its widely-discussed 2008 series *Black in America*, on July 22 and 23. Hosted by CNN anchor and special correspondent Soledad O'Brien, the original series aimed "to tell a story about black America that [would] focus on some of the more important aspects of black American life, concerning family, excelling in business, health care," Nelson explains. (Yousef 2009)

CNN has also recently considered bringing in big name minorities to appeal to the minority news market. For example, the *New York Post* has reported that the network is interested in wooing African-American entertainers, mentioning comedian Chris Rock and former "Talk Soup" host Aisha Tyler as possibilities. ("CNN Tries 'Diverse' Approach" 2010)

Jon Klein, the president of CNN's domestic networks, said he believed that CNN has a commitment to "reflect the country" (Lee 2008). As of 2012, CNN's hosts reflect his commitment: 39 percent are racial minorities, compared to 29 percent for MSNBC and 16 percent for FNC. In addition to hiring minority personalities to attract minority viewers, CNN has also let go of those not conducive to that goal. For example, Lou Dobbs was let go after nearly thirty years with the network. While the network was not clear on the reasons for his departure, many speculate that it stemmed from Dobbs's immigration stances and his reporting of the "birther" conspiracy theory.

As the cable news market stands in 2012, audiences have distinct choices. And, the networks have profited from following the ideologically segmented audience. By chasing the biggest ideological block of news viewers, Fox News has garnered and held onto the dominant positions for a decade. Fox News, particularly the evening programming, garners a mostly conservative audience while MSNBC, on the other hand, has a nearly homogenous liberal audience (Ladd 2012:69). This segmentation leaves different audiences with varying views of reality: "For the viewers who lean to the left of the ideological spectrum, they can watch MSNBC and rarely hear conservative voices; and the opposite goes for conservatives who watch Fox News Channel. This affords an exclusivity of thought that discourages debate and only serves to strengthen the divide between ideological sides" (Dagnes 2010). As media scholar Alison Dagnes (2010:xii) goes on to argue, "With so many media choices available, we have lost that communal feeling engendered by reading a hometown newspaper, listening to a national radio broadcast, or watching one of the three nightly network news programs on television. So many selections have led the media to become fragmented, polarized, and angry."

Broadcast News

The case of the cable news networks suggests that mass ideology has driven the distribution of the providers, as market-driven conceptions of news would suggest. Some might argue that the cable news networks are less news, and more entertainment. In this argument, if cable news networks follow market demands, it is not an abandonment of traditional norms of journalism because cable news really isn't intended to be traditional news in the first place. It is difficult to sustain this stance given that cable outlets serve the purpose of news whether their content is intended to be as traditional as older sources or not. But, it would be prudent to see if and how broad political opinions drive a source of news that is assumed to be more traditional. To do this, I return to the nightly network news data introduced in chapter 2.

This analysis compares mass levels of partisanship to issue coverage in the nightly network news over several decades. It will determine whether changing levels of party attachment in the audience lead news firms, generally thought to be traditional, to alter their substantive issue coverage. To ensure that the results of such a comparison speak to the effect of partisanship on issue coverage, this chapter accounts for the factors generally thought to affect news content: the real-world conditions and events that would drive the reporting of particular issues, the composition and actions of government, the topics discussed by national elites, and the audience's demand for specific sets of information. It is important to use systematic data for this inquiry because, unlike with the case study examining cable news above, the branding of the broadcast networks is much less overt, and therefore not necessarily visible in shorter snapshots or with case studies. More precise data is needed.

To operationalize mass partisanship, I employ a standard and long-used measure called "macropartisanship" (MacKuen et al. 1989). Like the time-series measures of news content described in chapter 2, the macropartisanship measure is in time-series format; this allows us to see how it fluctuates from quarter to quarter. The measure is drawn from aggregated public opinion polls asking national samples about partisanship using a standard question; the numerical measure is the percentage of Democratic party identifiers as a percentage of both major party identifiers. This is an ideal way to operationalize mass partisan preferences because (1) news firms may not be as interested in the raw percentage of either party's identifiers as in the proportion of one to the other and (2) this operationalization matters—the balance of government is often determined by the number of one party's identifiers in relation to the other party's (MacKuen et al. 1989).

In this study, macropartisanship has a mean of 56 and ranges from 51 to 64. This indicates that during the time period under study, the country was slightly more Democratic than Republican, and that macropartisanship fluctuated enough for reporters to be able to notice and adjust their reporting to follow it.

Given the variety of issues coded by the scheme introduced in chapter 2, one might ask which would be likely to be affected by changes in mass partisanship. What is the exact effect that this particular operationalization of gratification will have on news content? We would certainly not expect all issue areas to be affected by changes in macropartisanship. For example, we do not have a strong expectation that changes in the partisan balance in the audience would affect whether stories about transportation, technology, space travel, or foreign trade are reported or not.

These issues, like several others, do not have an overt partisan component to them; therefore a person's partisan attachment would probably not drive a desire to see those issues in the news. Of importance here is that partisanship should affect the reporting of issues that could, if only in the perceptions of newspeople, be seen to meet demands for gratification by partisan audiences.

To identify these issues, let me now introduce the concept of *party-owned issues.* Party-owned issues are those issue areas that previous research has found to be associated by the public with one of the parties (Petrocik et al. 2003; Budge and Farlie 1983). Polls over time demonstrate that the public views certain issues as associated with, and competently handled by, one party or the other (Petrocik 1996). For example, if asked what issues the Republicans are good at, most people would answer with a few particular issue areas; and if asked what issues the Democrats are good at, most people would answer with a few different particular issue areas. Parties have long-standing reputations about what they do, what they are good at, and what their brand signifies. Since the public identifies those issues with a particular party, that party is said to "own" those issues. Therefore, it is prudent to expect that news firms will vary the reporting of *party-owned* issues in response to changes in mass partisanship.

I note that this distinction does not imply that either party is in actuality better at handling the issues they own, only that each party is viewed by most people as having an association with those issues. Certainly, a hardcore partisan might say that his or her party of preference is better at *every* issue when compared to the other party. However, most people are not quite that rigid, and do at least give their least preferred party credit for having a long-standing association with certain issues. The Democrats have been found to "own" the issues of Civil Rights, Labor, and Social Welfare. The Republicans "own" Law & Crime and Defense.[1] No doubt, these distinctions are debatable. For example, during the Iraq and Afghanistan wars, many argued that the Democrats were much better at defense than the supposedly bumbling Republicans. But, in terms of long-standing reputations, if you were to ask any group of people what issues they associate with the two parties, the answers would look similar to the issues identified here.

Given this, a natural question arises: Are journalists aware of the party's long-standing issue reputations? Do journalists respond to these reputations in their reporting? The short answer is a resounding yes—scholarship has long demonstrated that reporters are aware of, and highly responsive to, the parties' issue advantages (Hayes 2005). For example, in a content analysis of campaign coverage, Petrocik et al. (2003) find that the parties' issue advantages lead to altered news coverage, and thus issue reporting reflects the "perceptions of the press about the issue agendas of the parties." Puglisi (2011) also shows that news firms modify their coverage on the basis of issue ownership: he finds that the *New York Times* reports party-owned issues in response to election cycles and the incumbents' party. Hayes (2008) shows that reporters alter the favorability of news coverage given to presidential candidates in response to the parties' issue-handling reputations: he finds that reporters cover presidential candidates more positively when they focus on issues their party "owns" rather than on other issues. So, journalists are aware of party-owned issues and they adjust coverage on the basis of those long-standing reputations. Now let's see if journalists adjust their reporting of party-owned issues to follow macropartisanship.

If the nightly news outlets do follow mass partisanship, changes in macropartisanship should lead to clear and identifiable changes in the reporting of issues. If the percentage of Republicans in the public were to increase, then the networks should subsequently report more Republican-owned issues in order to satisfy the demands of partisans. If the percentage of Democrats in the public were to increase, the networks should subsequently report more Democratic-owned issues. If reporters do not account for partisanship when constructing issue content, then party-owned issues would be reported invariant to changes in mass partisanship.

In this analysis, there are 12,802 Republican-owned issue stories and 2,556 Democratic-owned issue stories. This represents 15,358 total stories and 27 percent of the total issues coded during the time frame. The

airing of Republican and Democratic issues is not related to the airing
of the other: the correlation coefficient between the two is .02. In other
words, the proportions of Republican-owned and Democratic-owned
stories can increase or decrease at the same time, or not. Republican-
owned issues appear an average of 87 times per quarter with a range of 4
to 246. Democratic issues appear an average of 17 times per quarter with
a range of 0 to 83. As these numbers indicate, Republican-owned issues
appear more than Democratic-owned issues at a rate of about 5 to 1.

This might seem immediately amiss. If Democrats in the audience
tend to outnumber Republicans during the time period under study, why
would Republican-owned issues outnumber Democratic-owned issues
by such a wide margin? There are several reasons why this might be the
case. First, we have no theoretical reason to expect that the number of
stories reported about any particular issue areas would be similar. As
the data collection in chapter 2 demonstrates, some issues are reported
frequently while others are reported infrequently. We should not expect
balance between the number of Republican-owned and Democratic-
owned issues (or between any other issues for that matter). Second, multiple forces can affect the issue content of news programs; I would not
suggest that macropartisanship is the *only* force affecting content. And,
there are theoretical reasons already discussed suggesting that certain
issues should be reported more than others. Previous research suggests
that news firms focus on, and give precedence to, events that naturally
hold spectacle for audiences (Rosenstiel 2005; Hamilton 1998; Patterson
1994; Epstein 1981; Gans 1979; Tuchman 1978). As a result, those issue
areas that spectacular events typically fall into will receive pronounced
coverage. Events such as explosions, wars, murders, attacks, and trials
are those that hold spectacle for audiences and fit engrained routines.
These events typically comprise the Republican-owned issues of Defense
and Law & Crime. Therefore, we might expect Republican-owned issues
to be reported quite frequently. On the other hand, the events often
comprising Democratic-owned issues, Labor, Social Welfare, and Civil
Rights, are rarely so fantastic that they would, on their own, be considered newsworthy. Thus, we should expect Republican-owned issues to

be reported more often than Democratic-owned issues—but not necessarily because of partisan demands.

Does the disparity between Republican-owned issues and Democratic-owned issues affect the analysis? The simple answer is no. First, because this analysis is interested in the factors that lead to over-time fluctuation in the amount of owned issues reported, their absolute amounts or the disparity between their amounts is of lesser concern. Second, this analysis is interested in the factors that drive over-time variation, and therefore, this disparity does not suggest that macropartisanship does not affect issue coverage.

Now, it is prudent to compare macropartisanship to our measures of party-owned issues to see if one drives the other. In doing this, it is important to account for other factors that may affect the reporting of those party-owned issues. For example, if Congress decides to spend a year debating health care legislation, it is likely that news firms would cover health care– and social welfare–related issues—and this would probably have little to do with changes in macropartisanship. To be sure that any statistical relationship found between mass partisanship and issue coverage stems from the former causing the latter, researchers should account for the effects of events, conditions, policy, and elite rhetoric, as well as the public's issue concerns, on issue coverage in the news.

To begin, included in this investigation are measures of the public's issue concerns. As chapter 2 demonstrated, public issue concerns in some instances drive the reporting of issues. Thus, I want to parse out the effects of macropartisanship on news coverage from the effect of issue demands on news coverage. As in chapter 2, a time-series of Gallup's Most Important Problem question (MIP) is used to measure the percent citing Democratic-owned issues and the percent citing Republican-owned issues as the most important problem facing the nation each quarter. The percentage of the population identifying Republican-owned issues as the most important was an average of 19 percent; about 12 percent of the population on average identified Democratic issues as the most important.[2] If we were to observe the audience's demands for information driving issue coverage, then an increase in concern over Republican-owned (or Democratic-owned) issues would lead to an increase in the reporting of Republican-owned (or Democratic-owned) stories. If we were to observe agenda-setting, then Republican-owned (or Democratic-owned) stories would drive concern over Republican (or Democratic) issues.

In addition to the public's concerns, we must account for the effect that policymakers, policy, and actual events and conditions have on subsequent news content. Take news coverage of the 9/11 attacks, for example. The public did not have a large interest in Defense issues on 9/10/2001, and the major story across the country was a scandal involving congressman Gary Condit. But, when the terrorists killed three thousand people the next day, those attacks drew coverage of their own volition. In short, many forces drive news content besides public demands. If we want to say that correlations between news content and public opinion are valid indicators of audience influence over the news, we need to rule out the effect of other major forces.

With this said, statistical models cannot account for all of social reality; thousands of indicators would be necessary. However, analyses should account only for those indicators thought to be the most relevant to explaining the interplay between opinions and news. The following section details these indicators. With this said, I offer a word of caution: it would be a mistake for researchers to pick indicators according to their salience in the media. This might include, for instance, a variable denoting the 1995 O. J. Simpson murder trial because the researcher knew a priori that the trial was salient in the media. Such a strategy is tautological: stories that the researcher knew were salient in the media would be used to predict stories that were salient in the media. Therefore, I employ indicators that are, in some ways, "bland," and do not reflect specific stories that are known to have been reported.

To account for the actions and discourse of policymakers, I begin by measuring the president's party affiliation. The president and his actions receive a large amount of coverage in the news, and it is likely that (1) journalists would cover the president differently according to his party affiliation and (2) presidents of differing party affiliation are likely to speak and act on different issues, so the press would have different actions to cover. To directly account for the actions of the president, I include the number of executive orders each quarter addressing Democratic-owned issues compared to the number of executive orders addressing Republican-owned issues.[3] If the president, for example, were to issue a slew of executive orders addressing social welfare, we would expect reporters to report more stories on that issue area. To directly account for the effects that presidential discourse may have on the news agenda, I measure the number of mentions the president gives to Democratic- and Republican-owned issues, respectively, in the opening remarks of their press conferences each quarter. We should expect that if a president were to discuss Defense issues frequently, reporters would address Defense more often in response. And, given that elections dominate reporting prior to elections and crowd out much other substantive discussion, I measure whether a presidential election is taking place each quarter or not.

Congress may influence the issue areas addressed by reporters as well. If Congress were to consider major legislation, or pass a sweeping bill, the news would probably report this. Because journalists would be responding to Congress instead of to public demands in this case, we want to account for it. To account for congressional discourse, I include the number of House committee hearings addressing Democratic-owned issues minus the number of hearings that address Republican-owned issues each quarter. We might expect that if Congress were to discuss Defense or Social Welfare, for instance, then those issues would make it into the news agenda because of the congressional attention. I also account for congressional control—a Democratic House would probably address different issues than a Republican one—and this would probably drive the substance of available news. To track legislation that may affect reporting, I measure the passage of major legislation (according to *Congressional Quarterly*) addressing Democratic- and Republican-owned issues each quarter. We might expect that if Congress passed major legislation addressing Labor, for instance, reporters would probably report on that major legislation.

Now, I measure the events and conditions that may affect the reporting of each individual issue area. For Defense issues, I denote whether the United States is involved in an active ground war during each quarter and measure the number of troops killed in battle each quarter. To measure the conditions that would lead to Law & Crime reporting, I include a measure of national violent crime rates over time. Imagine if a war were to erupt, or crime rates were to spike—we would expect that reporters would address Defense and Law issues more prominently given the events taking place.

To account for the events and conditions that could affect the reporting of social welfare stories, I include the number of people receiving food stamp assistance and the percentage of people living below poverty levels each quarter. To account for the conditions that would lead to Civil Rights coverage, I include the levels of unemployment in the black community and the number of important civil rights Supreme Court decisions each quarter. To account for the events and conditions that would be likely to affect the reporting of Labor stories, I include measures of total unemployment and the number of work stoppages due to strikes each quarter. We could reasonably expect changes in these conditions on the ground—independent of public demands—to affect the stories journalists report.[4]

The analysis employs a statistical technique called vector-autoregression (VAR). VAR examines time-series data for statistical causation with a series of Granger causality tests (Brandt and Williams 2007). Thus, this analysis is not unlike the Granger analyses in chapter 2. But, unlike traditional bivariate Granger tests, VAR can include multiple endogenous and exogenous variables, it allows the retrieval of impulse-response functions that show how changes in one endogenous variable "shock," or affect, another over several periods, and it can serve as an all-purpose model. In short, VAR alleviates the problems of identifying a more specific model where the theories of interest are either imprecise or provide conflicting expectations—VAR allows the data to determine these relationships (Brandt and Williams 2007; Bartels 1991; Freeman et al. 1989; Sims 1980). In this case, current theories on audience influence

Table 3.1. Results of Vector Auto Regression

	Proportion of Democratic to Republican Issues in the News	Macropartisanship	Proportion of Democratic to Republican Issue Concerns
Macropartisanship Ll	.147* (.070)	.750* (.047)	.012 (.026)
Proportion of Democratic to Republican Issues in the News Ll	.042 (.058)	-.028 (.052)	.015 (.028)
Proportion of Democratic to Republican Issue Concerns Ll (Coefficient for control variables withheld)	.260 (.190)	.185 (.127)	.478* (.069)
Constant	-13.8* (4.7)	14.5* (3.15)	-1.75 (1.72)
r-square	.445	.967	.755
RMSE	1.1	.726	.398
Chi-square	116.1	4288.1	445.9
n	145	145	145

p values: *$\geq$.05. Full model is available upon request.

and media effects provide vague predictions of lag length, and theories of audience influence on news content provide a causal direction that is in direct conflict with theories of media effects. Tests on the data indicate that a lag length of one quarter is appropriate to use in this model; this makes intuitive sense as I expect profit-driven news firms to follow public opinion fairly closely—at no more than one quarter behind.

Table 3.1 displays the results (for the purpose of readability, the coefficients of our control variables are withheld but the full model is available upon request). Each dependent variable is listed in the columns at the top, and each independent variable is listed in the first column going downward. Coefficients with a star indicate statistical significance; the standard error is in parentheses below. Positive coefficients indicate a positive relationship while a negative coefficient indicates a negative one. I include three main endogenous or dependent variables in the model. The first is the time-series of party-owned issue coverage; I operationalize this as the percentage of Democratic-owned stories divided by the percent of Republican-owned stories aired each quarter. This is the variable I most want to explain—whether it is affected by macropartisanship, and how. Macropartisanship and the public's issue concerns are also included as dependent variables at the top. The variables representing real-world conditions, and the actions and discourse of government are treated as exogenous in the VAR model and are listed on the left.

With regard to the upper-most left coefficient, the lagged measure of macropartisanship significantly and positively affects the reporting of issues in the hypothesized direction. As the public becomes more Democratic, firms report more Democratic-owned issues in relation to Republican-owned issues, and as the public becomes more Republican, the news outlets report more Republican-owned issues in relation to Democratic-owned issues. More specifically, a one percentage point positive change in macropartisanship (the country turns more Democratic than Republican) leads to the reporting of four more Democratic-owned issues per quarter. This is a minor change. However, a ten-point Democratic shift in macropartisanship leads to an additional Democratic-owned story every other weekday; a twenty point shift leads to an additional story every weekday.

This represents an important effect given that (1) these results speak only to the top two stories each night, (2) these are the most influential stories in the broadcasts, and (3) traditional conceptions of journalism would not lead us to expect news firms to alter issue coverage in response to macropartisanship at all. This finding suggests rather strongly that news firms, even those considered to be stalwarts of traditional journalism, are not immune to the winds of public sentiment.

This effect is robust across model specification; models with different combinations of control variables, or no control variables, show similar effects. Not only does macropartisanship affect issue reporting at a one-quarter lag, as hypothesized, but it also has a lasting, albeit diminishing, effect. The model indicates that a one-unit change in macropartisanship significantly affects party-owned issue coverage in the news over three quarters. Mass partisanship appears to have a far-ranging impact on news content.[5]

Events, conditions, policy, and elite rhetoric also provide some, though not much, explanation for the reporting of party-owned issues in the news. Events do affect news coverage, i.e., the terror attacks of 9/11 were not reported until they actually happened. But studies have generally found a loose connection between the two. For example, reporters recently frenzied over the 2011 Casey Anthony murder trial—Ms. Anthony was accused of killing her daughter in Florida. But, during the same time, there were hundreds of murders and murder trials that received little or no national media coverage. This raises again the distinction between issues and events first discussed in chapter 2. News firms have discretion over which issues they emphasize; however, they competitively report *events* (e.g. Mason et al. 2001). Some events, such as the 9/11 attacks, are so relevant that news firms will have little discretion in choosing to report them. However, firms have even more discretion in *how* they cover the available set of events. Stories about the same event may address different issues. A nuclear arms treaty can be treated by reporters as a Defense issue, a foreign affairs issue, a government operations issue, or a technology issue. News firms can therefore follow audience-issue preferences with issue content because they have discretion to do so. This makes predicting issue coverage with conditions difficult, however.[6]

Returning to the results, the airing of party-owned issues does not affect mass partisanship. In line with previous scholarship addressing the endurance of partisan attitudes, macropartisanship has a unidirectional relationship with news content: it drives news content, and not vice versa. This is a particularly important point to note—scholars for years have faced difficulty trying to disentangle the causal direction between news content and audience opinions. The results in this model show a clear direction of affect, from audience to news. We see little evidence to suggest that the news is a propaganda machine that changes opinions in drastic fashion—market incentives prevent news firms from attempting to do this. Also, the data show that public issue concerns do not affect, nor are they affected by, party-owned issue reporting.[7]

Traditional conceptions of news suggest that mass partisanship should not affect the issues reported in the news, but the analysis suggests that it does. To be clear about these results, this analysis speaks to the effect of mass partisanship on broadcast network reporting of party-owned issues. Chapter 4 will demonstrate that other audience opinions drive news coverage as well.

Conclusion

This chapter addressed how audience demands for political gratification drive not only the news agenda but also the branding of entire mediums. First, a case study of cable news outlets showed how public demands drove the ideological branding and content of the three major cable outlets—CNN, FNC, and MSNBC. The outlets catering to the largest ideological segment of the audience receives the largest ratings. Second, a statistical analysis of the issues reported in the nightly network news shows that mass partisan attachments affect the reporting of even outlets considered to be traditional and immune from the immediate winds of public opinion.

To put these findings into context, let us return briefly to informational demands and the findings from chapter 2. If news firms follow audience demands for specific sets of information when constructing the news, this would indicate that the audience influenced content. However, this does not necessarily indicate that economic motives were involved: journalists may simply have responded to audiences as an expression of "civic-minded" journalism. In this, journalists report issues that the audience feels need resolutions. Civic-minded journalism is advocated by many as an important facet of democracy that increases news relevancy and can refocus government priorities (Bennett 2009; Journalists 2010; Peterson 1996). And, while providing a public good (information), this could also lead to higher profits as an unintended consequence, because firms would be meeting demands for that information (Rosenstiel et al. 2007). Audiences would watch the programs that provided the information they desired.

If news firms engaged in civic-minded journalism, then the audience's issue concerns would predict subsequent news coverage. For example, if the audience were to become highly concerned with public education, then news firms would provide news addressing that issue. In chapter 2, I demonstrated, as well, that public concerns over several broad issue areas drive subsequent coverage of those issues: news firms do follow audiences' demands for information in constructing their content. The evidence showing that news outlets meet demands for information does not necessarily indicate profit-driven journalism; firms may meet informational demands to be civic-minded.

However, profit seeking undoubtedly occurs when news firms follow either the audience's preferences for entertainment or the audience's preferences for gratification. It could not be argued that catering to these demands provides civic-minded journalism—meeting these demands does little good for society or for the individuals. In short, the difference between civic-minded and profit-driven journalism is not in the content of any particular story or stories, but rather in the *motivations* that lead to the reporting of those stories.

This study's results suggest that mass partisanship predicts issue coverage. Specifically, the results show that an increase in Democratic identification in the public leads to the reporting of more Democratic-owned issues (Civil Rights, Labor, and Social Welfare), while an increase in Republican identification in the public leads to the reporting of more Republican-owned issues (Defense and Law & Crime). These results suggest that profit motives affect substantive content even in traditional outlets: the audience's perceived desires for political gratification appear to drive issue content in the nightly network news. It is unclear whether this strategy pays dividends for news firms—for now, though, it is sufficient to show that news firms do partake in this behavior; the actual advantage gained is of less immediate importance.

Issue emphasis in the news has important institutional consequences: it can set the public agenda and prime citizens' evaluations of candidates. The reporting of "owned" issues is particularly important because these issues are likely to shift voter preference toward the "owning" party. This study shows how one factor, mass partisanship, leads to the reporting of owned issues by the networks.

On one hand, both chapter 2 and chapter 3 present evidence suggesting that news firms react to the public's concerns, thus indicating civic-minded journalism: news firms report the substantive issues that citizens believe are important. While not without its criticisms, this form of journalism provides some good for democracy. The press does pay attention to audiences and what audiences are thinking about.

On the other hand, the finding that mass ideology and partisanship predict news coverage is highly troubling. A free press is essential to democracy; however, a press cannot be "free" if it is dependent upon following audience predispositions. In the case of the cable news networks, the distribution of ideology in the audience appears to have branded the entire market. We cannot think that a media industry organized by the distribution of public opinion can be independent.

Journalists are not independent from market concerns. Scholars have long warned about the effect of public polling and mass attitudes on journalism (Gollin 1980; Ladd 1980; Van Hoffman 1980). While the American press may be free from much government interference, the economics of news may not only suppress issues that the public *needs* to know, in exchange for issues that the public *wants* to know, but may also brand entire news markets. Chapter 4 builds on the findings in this chapter by examining a broader range of opinions and news outlets.

4

Perpetual Feedback

Monitoring the New Media Environment

I want to make enough money so I can afford you. It's really that simple. You need to, in effect, help me by being a journalist that focuses on what our readers want and therefore generates more revenue. . . . [I]f we don't have the revenue, it doesn't really matter.
—Sam Zell, January 31, 2008

News outlets' incentives in the free market are clear: appeal to audiences with content that meets demand. If audiences consistently demanded information on critical topics that made them informed citizens, this would be great. News content would consistently meet democratic ideals and improve citizenship. Unfortunately, audience demands are not always so upright. People prefer content deviating greatly from the democratic ideal—and journalists know it. In response to the above remark by Sam Zell, owner of the *Chicago Tribune*, the *Los Angeles Times*, and several other newspapers, one of his journalists retorted, "But, what readers want are puppy dogs."

The incentives of the market do not care whether the news meets democratic ideals—the incentives merely encourage owners and operators like Sam Zell to meet demands and subsequently turn a profit. So, if news firms have to report puppy dogs, scurrilous sex scandals, or other trivial stories to meet demands, then that is all that matters to the market. There is no built-in incentive to produce news content that meets democratic ideals—only news that meets demands, whatever those demands might be. Financial incentives and intense competition lead news firms to chase the most prevalent audience demands—demands that currently, and unfortunately, are at odds with the requirements of democratic citizenship. Because of this, and as former CBS news director Fred Friendly claims, "Television makes so much [money] at its worst that it can't afford to do its best."

Chapters 2 and 3 argue that the public's opinions, namely, issue concerns, ideology, and partisanship, drive not only news content but also the branding of the entire cable news market. While vitally important, these opinions on their own cannot drive coverage of the thousands of events that come across news desks each day—many events are so unique it is difficult to predict exactly how audiences will want them covered. There may be no clear indication how audiences might react to certain stories, even knowing their partisanship, ideology, issue concerns, and other demographics. Therefore, news firms must find ways to solicit up-to-the-minute audience opinions on more finite matters in order to meet more specific demands in the dynamic news environment.

In the past, the overwhelming cost of soliciting a broad range of opinions on a daily basis would have put news firms out of business. Firms would have had to resort to telephone polls or in-person interviews; the cost of repeatedly getting large enough samples of respondents would have required enormous investments, and the results would have been less than timely. This is not to say that news firms did not use polls or other methods to learn about their audiences. But, firms were forced to rely on data that may have been weeks or months old, and spoke to only more general opinions rather than opinions about specific stories. Stories come and go rather quickly, and the money and resources needed in the past to commission polls or other sources of data on audience preferences for every emerging story would be immense. But, to the relief of news firm ownership, modern technology has solved this problem.

With modern technology, news firms now have the ability to solicit thousands of viewer opinions on moment-specific topics. News firms can get immediate feedback on their stories and use that feedback to shape future coverage. The mechanisms for soliciting audience feedback provide a widely available public sphere for audiences—and audiences have been seemingly happy to contribute. But, under the auspices of taking part in a public sphere, audiences have been too willing to provide firms with market information. This has made news firms much better able to target audiences; this is not unlike walking into a car dealership and telling the salesman which car you "just can't live without" before you begin to negotiate for it. And more broadly, the temptations created by increased market knowledge have further retarded the opportunities and incentives for journalists to use independent judgment.

This chapter begins with a discussion of the increasingly accurate and accessible methods used by news firms to monitor audience preferences. These include traditional ratings information, polling, as well as methods of tracking audience feedback and interest on individual stories. I then provide telling examples showing how news firms' solicitation of audience opinion shifts subsequent coverage. Afterwards, I allow news content to speak for itself, and demonstrate how both hard and softer news programs have met demands for entertainment by expending precious news space on meaningless but entertaining stories. Demands for entertainment lead not only to an overabundance of stories about trivial topics but also to a perverse style of reporting important stories.

Methods for Monitoring the Market

In recent years, news firms have embraced technologies that allow immediate audience feedback on their programming and reporting. Newspeople solicit audience feedback via email, Twitter, Facebook, text messages, and webpages. Audiences are encouraged to "keep the conversation going" after the report is over. Newspapers have for the last two decades published their stories on the internet, and in doing so have offered online readers methods for immediately responding to articles.

Readers can comment through online portals that allow newspapers to immediately see other readers' feedback. Historically, audiences have sent newspapers letters to the editor to comment on the reporting, and many newspapers employed an ombudsman to mediate between audience concerns over reporting and journalists. But currently, the speed and ease with which audiences can now respond to news is instantaneous and effortless. Readers no longer need to write a letter, stamp an envelope, and wait. Instead, audiences can now type their response directly into an online portal and send it in seconds. This not only provides the reader with the instant satisfaction of having provided feedback to the reporter and entered into the public sphere, but it also provides instant audience reviews for the outlet.

Newer and more efficient methods of gathering audience feedback provide news outlets with incredibly detailed information about how well their reporting has been received. And, in response, outlets can report the stories with the best and most feedback while reporting fewer stories receiving poor or scarce feedback. The economic incentives are there, and the potential is easy to see. Let's briefly examine the methods that news firms use to monitor the demands of the market.

Ratings

News outlets incur profits by selling space to other companies so they can advertise their products. Advertisers want to market their products to the largest segment of potential customers possible. How can companies know how many people they will reach when advertising on a particular media outlet? In the case of print media, news outlets can point to circulation rates. In the case of online media, outlets can track the number of hits particular pages receive as well as the IP addresses of those viewing the pages. But, with televised programming, it is slightly more difficult to track viewership. This is where independent rating agencies come in. Nielsen, perhaps the most popular, estimates how many and which types of people watch particular programming; they then provide this information to media outlets and advertisers. Ratings data then set the rates that advertisers are willing to pay for advertising space. News programming attracting large target audiences will be able to charge more for their advertising space than news programming reaching fewer people.

Ratings therefore give media firms important information for drawing in larger audiences. In response to ratings, media firms offer more programming generating high ratings, and less programming generating lower ratings. Highly rated television programming stays on the air, while poorly rated programs either disappear or are altered in an attempt to draw in higher ratings. This is certainly true with entertainment programming: nighttime shows disappear each season (sometimes midseason) as ratings information becomes available. Sit-coms and dramas are offered renewal contracts at the end of each season because of their ratings. News programming is little different. The cable news outlets, as discussed in chapter 3, have made many changes to their line-ups in response to poor ratings. Shows hosted in the last decade by Phil Donahue, Allan Keyes, and Elliot Spitzer are now gone. Shows that top the ratings, such as *The O'Reilly Factor*, stay.

Nielsen ratings rely on samples of households for estimating audience size and composition. While the ratings are a useful baseline for estimation, they are not without their shortcomings. As media analyst Arash Amel states (Anders 2010),

There has never been a proven method of actually measuring how many people are watching, for how long and what [they're watching]. It's all a shorthand that was created from a panel of several thousand homes, who were supposed to be indicative of 100 million television households, and to create some kind of a common ground so you could sell advertising. . . . It's just an immense amount of guesswork, that's carried out from a very small percentage, no matter how accurately you can say that each panel member is indicative of a certain amount of a demographic, no matter how closely you can vet that panel, you still don't know. . . . This is just [designed] for linear broadcasting, when you used to have three channels. Now take that, multiply it by a thousand—or how many cable channels you receive—then throw in a DVR. . . . All of this guesswork, over the past few decades, has basically been standardized as fact. But it's not.

Nielsen attempts to provide a great deal of specific information to both advertisers and programmers, but obtaining accurate information is no easy task in the current splintered market. Nielsen has excelled at providing broader demographic trends. But, it is far more difficult to obtain information about more specific aspects of programming and more specific opinions held by audiences. For example, viewers may prefer one news program to another, but which parts of the program do they like most, and, why? This is where news outlets will turn to other methods of gathering information about audience preferences.

Scientific Polls

Public polling provides information to media outlets about population demographics and opinions (political and otherwise). Polls for years have asked about partisanship, ideology, support for the president, interest in politics, policy concerns, and policy preferences. Media firms have access to these polls, and have taken to reporting them as news stories in and of themselves over the last few decades. In fact, most campaign coverage is now characterized by coverage of new poll results.

But public polling is not simply fodder for filling news space; it sends clear signals to news producers about the political opinions of the audience. As both chapters 2 and 3 demonstrated, the audience's opinions can affect the shape of subsequent programming. These polls were once expensive and time-consuming, but as Frank Newport, editor-in-chief of the Gallup Poll, explains, they have become far cheaper and more time efficient (2004:276):

Technological advances make it much simpler than it used to be for interested persons to conduct polls. Specialized companies can provide various poll components "off the shelf" cheaply and efficiently, allowing anyone who so desires to quite easily "do a poll" without much training or experience. Additionally, the Internet now provides a handy database of millions of potential poll respondents, and it is necessary to reach only a small fraction of them to conduct a poll. Robotic computers can call thousands of phone numbers and conduct interviews by having respondents punch in their answers, allowing those interested in conducting a poll to obviate the cost of live human interviewers.

The technological advances of the last three decades have indeed made the gathering of information far easier than before. Commenting on the newer techniques for gathering public opinion data, political scientist John Geer adds, "These techniques make it easier and cheaper to gather information quickly. Polling was revised again with the advent of computer technology in the 1980s, which allowed for quick data gathering and reporting. During that decade, the number of polling firms tripled, reflecting a seemingly insatiable appetite for rapid delivery of public opinion information" (2004:428). The end result is that news firms can track opinion dynamics very closely and adjust particular programming to bring it in line with those opinions, sometimes very quickly.

Unscientific Polls

Given advances in technology, news firms have been able to read public opinion through the use of nonscientific polling methods as well. Nonscientific polls do not offer the accuracy, reliability, or superior design of scientifically designed poll questions utilizing random selection, but they offer instantaneous responses to current questions and obtain responses only from those who watch the programming (this makes the polling relatively costless and the results at least somewhat indicative of base audiences). Much information about audiences can be gleaned from such poll questions: the distribution of responses can signal unanimity and strength of opinion, and the quantity of responses can signal interest in the topic. Cable news programs have been using audience polling as a way to get opinions for several years, and its use has increased. Cable networks employ survey questions several times a day.

For example, even the hard news show featured on FNC, *Special Report*, asks frequent questions of its audience. One might guess that this program would be driven more by traditional journalistic standards than other shows on the network, but it employs surveys to track audience opinions as much as, if not more than, softer shows such as *The O'Reilly Factor*. The results of these polls are often not surprising given the political make-up of FNC's audience: largely conservative and Republican. For example,

> We asked you how will the Supreme Court vote on Obamacare? And three percent said uphold all of it, 83 percent said reject all of it, and 14 percent said reject just the mandate. You might have been swayed by the panel a little bit. Thanks so much for your votes. We had more than 8,000 in this unscientific poll. (Bream, FNC [6:00] p.m., March 28, 2012)

FNC's audience had clear opinions about President Obama's Affordable Care Act—they were overwhelmingly against it in poll after poll. Given this, the imbalanced response to the question above should not come as a shock. Other questions, however, are designed to solicit opinions about matters that may not necessarily have a clear ideological or partisan bend to them. This is where soliciting audiences becomes particularly valuable—outlets may not have much leverage in guessing how audiences will want every story handled just from ideology, partisanship, and demographics. For example, airport security screenings began rolling out new body-scanning technology at checkpoints in 2010. On one hand, FNC's conservative audience could applaud measures to stop terrorism; on the other hand, that same audience might be wary of having their rights infringed upon by a government agency. As a guide to better target their reporting to their audience's opinions, FNC asked several questions over the years regarding this topic. As the below example shows, some of the questions tried to assess audience opinions in interesting ways: "We asked you in our text to vote poll tonight, have you been inappropriately touched during airport screenings? And 48 percent of you said yes, 52 percent responded no. Thank you for your votes" (Baier, FNC [6:00] p.m., May 9, 2012).

Other polls on FNC's *Special Report* focus on topics that may divide Republicans and conservatives—FNC's primary audience. In these cases, gleaning audience opinions can provide direction to producers in choosing how to address intraparty questions. "We asked you which presidential candidate has the most intriguing spouse. And 16 percent said Newt Gingrich, seven percent said Ron Paul, 56 percent said Mitt Romney, and 21 percent said Rick Santorum. Thank you for your votes. We had more than 6,000 of them tonight" (Baier, FNC [6:00] p.m., March 21, 2012).

FNC's *O'Reilly Factor* strategically uses polls as well. I begin with an example prior to the 2008 election in which Barack Obama handily won the presidency over Republican John McCain. Given that that election was characterized as a blowout, one can see that those responding to the poll were probably not representative of the population (even Bill O'Reilly seems aware of this).

> Here are the results of Billoreilly.com poll, which asked if you have to predict today who will win, McCain 66, Obama 34. Now I think that may be an emotional reaction to the poll. It's *not a scientific poll*. Every other poll shows Obama in the lead. But we'll see. Maybe "The Factor" viewers are more perspicacious. (O'Reilly, FNC [8:00] p.m., October 13, 2008; emphasis added)

But unlike the poll above where the questions seem to measure little more than the general dispositions of the target audience, other polls solicit opinions on matters that are not necessarily so clearly partisan or ideological at the outset. For example, in 2012 a tragic shooting occurred in Florida. An unarmed teenager, Trayvon Martin, was shot and killed by a neighborhood watch captain, George Zimmerman. Over a series of months, the case garnered increasing media exposure and was a frequent topic on *The O'Reilly Factor*. But, as the case initially gained notoriety, it was not immediately clear how partisans and ideologues would interpret the evidence. As O'Reilly was able to ascertain, the case was not only resonating with viewers, given the number of responses to his poll question, but also his audience was not convinced of Zimmerman's culpability in the shooting. "We asked you at this point, based upon what you've seen, do you believe George Zimmerman will be convicted of second-degree murder. Nearly 25,000 voted. Ninety-one percent say no; nine percent say yes" (O'Reilly, FNC [8:00] p.m., May 22, 2012).

In keeping with the opinions of his audience, O'Reilly's coverage was, in comparison to that of other networks, very sympathetic to Zimmerman's defense. MSNBC's progressive audience was not sympathetic to Zimmerman, and as a result, the coverage on that network was initially highly inflammatory, particularly from host Al Sharpton. However, as the facts released by investigators began to suggest that Zimmerman acted in self-defense, MSNBC drastically decreased its coverage of the case.

In addition to polls about current opinions, O'Reilly uses polls on occasion to gauge audience preferences about the actions of usually famous people. He calls this segment "Pinhead or Patriot." Audience members vote on whether the person is a pinhead or not, and from these votes, O'Reilly can gauge how his audience views particular actions. Traditional journalism would not call for news programming to solicit opinions such as this—and even conceptions of civic-minded journalism would not consider such voting valuable. This type of audience surveying serves only to provide information about audiences to news producers. For example,

> Now, last night we showed you New York Yankees star Alex Rodriguez being fed popcorn by the actress Cameron Diaz. That was captured for the world at the Super Bowl. How lucky for them both. Seventy-two percent of you think Mr. Rodriguez is a pinhead for eating popcorn in that manner. Twenty-eight percent say he is a patriot. And I believe old Alex will be subject to a lot of popcorn jokes this coming season. (O'Reilly, FNC [8:00] p.m., February 9, 2011)

With "Pinheads and Patriots," audiences think they are merely voicing their opinion—perhaps on something trivial—and they are. But they are also providing endless sources of data to O'Reilly's producers that can be used for shaping future content. FNC is not alone in this endeavor; for example, MSNBC's Ed Schultz has taken to frequent audience polling as well. One difference we might note about Schultz's questions is that the wording of many of them is highly inflammatory, and as a result, they nearly always have lopsided outcomes. This diminishes the value of many of the questions, but MSNBC can still measure interest by the number of responses to each question. From the results, we can see the political tilt of MSNBC's audience, which is opposite that of Fox.

> Welcome back to THE ED SHOW. Tonight in our survey, I asked you who is dividing the country? Ninety five percent say Mitt Romney; five percent say President Obama. (Dyson, MSNBC [8:00] p.m., May 4, 2012)

> ED SHOW survey tonight, I asked is the Ryan Republican budget immoral? Ninety eight percent of you said yes; two percent of you said no. (Schultz, MSNBC [8:00] p.m., April 26, 2012)

The responses to the above questions suggest the strength and unanimity of opinion present in the MSNBC audience. Other questions elicit slightly less lopsided responses from audience members. In these cases, MSNBC can learn where there is less agreement among audience members and tread more carefully with those stories: "Tonight in our survey, I asked you is it fair game to discuss a candidate's religious beliefs? Sixty three percent of you say yes; 37 percent of you say no" (Schultz, MSNBC [8:00] p.m., May 18, 2012).

Polling has changed in the last three decades. Most importantly, it has become less expensive and more efficient. For news firms wanting to measure opinion on a daily basis regarding dynamic and emerging stories, new methods of polling present a window into the audience never before imagined. Now, let's turn to examine how innovations in social media have also been used by news firms to gather audience opinions.

Social Media

In addition to advances in opinion polling, social media have revolutionized the media's ability to read audience preferences. Viewers are asked to go online and follow the hosts and reporters. News firms ask that audiences "continue the conversation" online in social mediums such as Facebook and Twitter. This gives news outlets nearly unlimited access to audience opinions, and they can monitor audience opinions in these open forums without having to use restrictive questions. The invitations to share opinions in this manner have become so commonplace, few people even notice how new and strange it is when compared to news just a decade ago. For example, typical solicitations for feedback from *The Ed Show* and *Anderson Cooper 360*:

> And you can follow me on twitter @edshow and you can like "the Ed Show" on Facebook. We're coming right back. Stay with us. (Schultz, MSNBC [8:00] p.m., June 4, 2012)

> Let us know what you think. We're on Facebook. Follow me on Twitter @AndersonCooper. We will be tweeting over this hour. (Cooper, CNN [8:00] p.m., June 19, 2012)

These invitations to social network with the news outlets provide a great deal of useful feedback. Audiences can tell the outlets exactly what they like and don't like about the product—and there is little cost for such feedback. Consider that in the restaurant business, restaurants have to incentivize customers to fill out online surveys or call into customer-feedback hotlines. For news outlets, the customers—the audience—provide feedback with no incentives provided to them. News firms can essentially tap a gold mine of customer feedback, and this feedback drives coverage.

For example, the FNC show *Special Report* allows viewers to choose the issues it will discuss. This gives audience direct say over their information environment, and also provides news outlets with the ability to provide audiences with the stories they want on a segment-by-segment basis.

> Every week viewers vote for your choice online in our *Friday lightning round* poll. This week federal bonuses won, 60 percent of you voted for that. So let's talk about it with the panel. We are talking about $400 million in federal bonuses last year. OK or not OK? (Bream, FNC [6:30] p.m., May 18, 2012)

While audience members are happy to "keep the conversation going," they are somewhat unaware of the vast amounts of information they provide to news producers. In addition to conversing though social media websites, news outlets can also solicit audience opinions efficiently through email portals. As new events occur, news firms ask audiences to send in their thoughts. More so than fixed-answer poll questions and short social media posts, viewer letters allow news producers to obtain a more qualitative and in-depth view of audience opinion. Viewer mail has become a large part of news programming, and in many cases viewer mail serves as news itself. Beyond providing news outlets with fodder to fill on-air space, the thousands of letters received provide rich data for understanding the demands of audiences. In the case of *The O'Reilly Factor*, Bill O'Reilly gives audiences an open call for email feedback, and audiences respond to the range of stories covered on the show. Unlike other outlets that read the letters, some perhaps on the air, O'Reilly engages with audience opinions by responding to many of the letters.

> Now, the mail. Kristen Poulos, North Chelmsford, Massachusetts. "Bill, a person is not a bigot for disagreeing with gay marriage, but groups that attack homosexuals for their lifestyles are haters. Very disappointed in your 'Talking Points' analysis."

Why, Kristen? I simply said the states should decide the issue based upon what standards the folks want. President Obama agrees with me, so what's the beef? (O'Reilly, FNC [8:00] p.m., May 11, 2012)

Much like modern televised news programs, the online versions of newspapers and other news sources now come equipped with portals for readers to post comments. Editors can see how many comments each story solicits, and how many people clicked on each story. This undoubtedly drives newspeople to focus on topics that "bring in the clicks." It is on rare occasions that outlets do not allow readers to comment; some of these occur when the outlet knows that the news item is out of step with public opinion. The following example is from the *New York Times'* Paul Krugman (2011).

What happened after 9/11—and I think even people on the right know this, whether they admit it or not—was deeply shameful. The atrocity should have been a unifying event, but instead it became a wedge issue. Fake heroes like Bernie Kerik, Rudy Giuliani, and, yes, George W. Bush raced to cash in on the horror. And then the attack was used to justify an unrelated war the neocons wanted to fight, for all the wrong reasons.

A lot of other people behaved badly. How many of our professional pundits—people who should have understood very well what was happening—took the easy way out, turning a blind eye to the corruption and lending their support to the hijacking of the atrocity? The memory of 9/11 has been irrevocably poisoned; it has become an occasion for shame. And in its heart, the nation knows it. I'm not going to allow comments on this post, for obvious reasons.

It was not difficult to tell that Krugman's analysis was out of step with most Americans' opinions on the tenth anniversary of 9/11; even the *New York Times'* liberal audience would probably be incensed. This is probably why opinions such as this one make only rare appearances in major news sources. But now that we have seen the mechanisms for gauging opinion, we must ask, What are the specific effects those opinions have on coverage?

The Effect on News Coverage

Polls and other methods of soliciting feedback allow news firms to track audience opinions, and from there, shape subsequent coverage so as to draw in larger audiences. The following case studies demonstrate a few examples of this. While the previous two chapters employed large-scale statistical analyses, a series of individual case studies may be more valuable here. This is the case because I want to capture the nuance of the interplay between very specific audience opinions and specific aspects of coverage. I begin with coverage of criminal trials on FNC's *The O'Reilly Factor*—to show how journalistic standards of reporting change in response to audience demands.

Host Bill O'Reilly devotes a good portion of his program to covering salient and controversial criminal trials. O'Reilly makes it clear in much of his coverage that his purpose is never to "try the case" on television but rather to inform "the folks" about the latest developments. This seems like fine journalistic practice, and it is. Unfortunately, O'Reilly only seems to follow this rule when his Republican and conservative audience is sympathetic to the accused.

In 2006, members of the Duke University lacrosse team were accused of raping a black stripper in their campus house. Many at Duke University and in the media were quick to presuppose the guilt of the three accused white college students. Liberal media outlets along with liberal professors took the accuser's story at face value. O'Reilly's audience, mainly conservative, Republican, and white, was more likely to find the accused students sympathetic. O'Reilly's discussion during his coverage followed the probable opinions of his audience:

> Now for the top story tonight, convicting two Duke lacrosse players in the court of public opinion. Obviously, that's before any evidence is presented in court. Is that fair? You have two young boys, 20 years old, who may be innocent. And they must be given the presumption of innocence. They must in a just society. (O'Reilly, FNC [8:00] p.m., April 20, 2006)

O'Reilly in this and other segments argued that the Duke players should not be tried on television. Beginning in 2008, the United States Justice Department began to investigate Maricopa County, Arizona, sheriff Joe Arpaio for civil rights violations. Arpaio, a Republican, had gained notoriety for being tough on crime, prisoners, and illegal immigration. At the time, Arpaio was gaining popularity with the Right because of his outspokenness on the issue of illegal immigration and also because he appeared a martyr in the face of federal investigation. In keeping with his audience's dispositions, O'Reilly again cautioned against trying the case in the media: "Sheriff Joe Arpaio in Arizona being sued by the federal government for racial profiling. Now, I don't want to try this thing on TV, but what does the government want out of this?" (O'Reilly, FNC [8:00] p.m., May 10, 2012).

As previously mentioned, in 2012, George Zimmerman was being prosecuted for the second-degree murder of Trayvon Martin, an unarmed teenager. Liberals and liberal news outlets provided coverage that appeared to prejudge the guilt of Zimmerman. O'Reilly noted this in his coverage, and continued to reject trying cases in the media. One might have suspected that O'Reilly's audience would be sympathetic to Zimmerman, and O'Reilly's own polling suggested that they were (a previously mentioned poll showed that 91 percent of respondents thought that Zimmerman would be found not guilty).

> So you know that I have been criticizing people who convict George Zimmerman on TV. I'm sure you know that right? You convicted him in print of cold blooded murder. Don't you have any hesitation? Don't you see that that's not right? (O'Reilly, FNC [8:00] p.m., April 3, 2012)

> We just said let the system work. Let's not convict this Zimmerman on television. Let's not make the wild charges. (O'Reilly, FNC [8:00] p.m., April 12, 2012)

But, what would seem to be the application of good journalistic principles in the above cases becomes discarded as soon as the audience is not so sympathetic to the defendant. Take, for instance, former Democratic vice-presidential nominee and senator John Edwards. Edwards was accused of illegally diverting campaign funds to pay off his pregnant mistress (while his wife was undergoing treatment for cancer). The trial took place in spring 2012. In the following discussion with legal analyst Megyn Kelly, O'Reilly abandoned his earlier norms. He convicted Edwards not only of diverting campaign funds but also of being worse than homicidal terrorists.

> BILL O'REILLY: OK, John Edwards, he's got to be the worst guy in the world. There's nobody worse than this guy. . . . Got to be in the top three.
>
> MEGYN KELLY: Jose Padilla is probably a little worse.
>
> BILL O'REILLY: You know what? If I had a choice, I think I'd take Padilla. Really.
>
> MEGYN KELLY: Really? Somebody who wants to set up a dirty bomb in the United States or somebody who had an affair.
>
> BILL O'REILLY: Padilla is an idiot. Padilla is an ignoramus, all right, and he's a crazy guy. Edwards, vice-presidential candidate. Wife has cancer. Doing all of this crazy stuff. (O'Reilly, Kelly, FNC [8:00] p.m., May 3, 2012)

> BILL O'REILLY: But I have to tell the audience, I mean, we were on to Edwards very, very early here on "The Factor." We knew that this guy was a sleazy hombre, dishonest and all of that. So I don't feel sorry for him.
>
> MEGYN KELLY: Sleazy hombre?
>
> BILL O'REILLY: Yes. "Hombre" is "man" in Spanish. Sleazy. I don't know how to say sleazy in Espanol. If you know, let me know. But he is a sleazy hombre and always has been. And he's a dishonest guy, and this is a karma play. (O'Reilly, Kelly, FNC [8:00] p.m., April 12, 2012)

The most pertinent question of the Edwards trial was whether or not Edwards knew about the campaign funds that were diverted to his mistress in exchange for her silence. O'Reilly was convinced that Edwards knew about the payments, and thus he was ready to convict: "He knew about them. Are you kidding me. . . . Guilty, guilty, guilty and guilty" (O'Reilly, FNC [8:00] p.m., May 10, 2012).

Despite the fact that O'Reilly pronounced Edwards guilty, the trial turned out to be rather complicated and technical. In the end, Edwards was not convicted on any of the six felony charges against him and the Justice Department declined to pursue the charges further. The episode suggests that O'Reilly decided to "convict" Edwards on air and violate what had become a journalistic norm for him, because Edwards was on the opposite side of the political fence as his audience. The political sensibilities of his audience drove not only content but also, in this case, the application of journalistic standards.

Some might disagree, and instead suggest that because Edwards had had an unsavory affair while his wife was receiving chemotherapy, O'Reilly felt compelled to convict him on-air. Certainly, many people would find Edwards's adultery objectionable whether he had misused campaign funds or not. This may have driven O'Reilly's actions. Perhaps, O'Reilly's coverage of the Jerry Sandusky trial may shed light on this. Sandusky was a former Penn State football coach who was put on trial and eventually found guilty of molesting young boys. Most would agree that child molestation is more objectionable than adultery or misuse of campaign funds. But, in discussing the Sandusky child molestation trial, O'Reilly said, "I don't want to convict the guy on television" (O'Reilly, FNC [8:00] p.m., June 15, 2012).

Given this, it appears that O'Reilly reports criminal trials differently according to the political identity of the accused, presumably to satisfy the political preconceptions of his audience. While it is good journalism to presuppose the innocence of the accused, it is not good journalism to pick and choose, on the basis of audience opinions, whom to give that benefit of the doubt to.

Now let us look at a case in which news personalities had to change their coverage of a particular topic due to feedback from the audience. Christine O'Donnell, a Republican, fought and won a hotly contested primary battle for an open Senate seat in Delaware in 2010. O'Donnell was a favorite of Tea Party backers, while her opponent, Mike Castle, was a long-time establishment Republican. Polls suggested a tight race between O'Donnell and Castle for the nomination, but polls also showed that Castle had a strong shot at winning the general election while O'Donnell would face an uphill battle. Upon O'Donnell's primary victory on September 14, two Fox News contributors, Karl Rove and Charles Krauthammer, painted less than flattering portraits of O'Donnell. Beginning with Rove's comments:

> One thing that Christine O'Donnell is now going to have to answer in the general election that she didn't have to answer in the primary is her own checkered background. . . . You made out a list of the things that Mike Castle had done wrong. You didn't make out a list of the things that Christine O'Donnell had done right. I've met her. I got to tell you, I wasn't frankly impressed at her abilities as a candidate. And again, these serious questions about how does she make her living? Why did she mislead voters about her college education? How come it took nearly two decades to pay her college bills so she could get her college degree? How did she make a living? Why did she sue a well-known and well—conservative think tank? Did you ask her about the people who were following her home to her headquarters and how she has checked each night in the bushes? Did you ask her—I mean, there were a lot of nutty things she has been saying that just simply don't add up. . . . This is not a race we're going to be able to win. (Rove, FNC [6:00] p.m., September 14, 2010)

> I think O'Donnell is going to be a weak candidate. I'm not sure how much influence they would have if elected in the caucus. I mean overall, people have to decide do you want to follow the Buckley rule and get elected? And in Delaware, that candidate was Castle. He won 12 times statewide. She has lost twice, O'Donnell has lost twice.
>
> I think it's probably a lost seat and it could cost them the majority. (Krauthammer, FNC [6:00] p.m., September 15, 2010)

O'Donnell's victory in the primary was seen as a huge victory for the Tea Party movement, and many were very excited—especially in FNC's audience. But, as Rove's and Krauthammer's comments suggest, her candidacy seemed doomed to ultimate failure—polling showed her lagging far behind her Democratic opponent. Despite this, both Rove and Krauthammer were lambasted in letters and other social media communications from their audiences. In response to the negative audience feedback, both commentators softened their stance on O'Donnell during the following weeks to become more in line with their audience's opinion on the matter. Initially, both commentators addressed on-air why their commentary strayed from the audience's. In addressing the email onslaught he received, Krauthammer back-peddled:

KRAUTHAMMER: Yes. I profited mightily on my stance on Christine O'Donnell. . . . (Laughter). . . . And that was a good start for her. I hope—I think her chances are very, very long, maybe Detroit Lions long, but I hope she wins.

BRET BAIER: Send them to your email right?

CHARLES KRAUTHAMMER: I'll give you my home address. (Baier, Krauthammer, FNC [6:00] p.m., September 20, 2012)

Krauthammer appeared on The O'Reilly Factor the next evening to further discuss his disjuncture with his audience.

BILL O'REILLY: So what kind of mail are you getting on this, Charles?

CHARLES KRAUTHAMMER: I'd say it's decidedly negative, Bill. . . . I'm sitting in my office, and my assistant comes in and says "You look tired." I said, "Yes, I'm a little bit tired." He says, "Are you tired? I've been reading your mail. I'm exhausted. I can't read any more." And it's been pretty heavy. . . .

BILL O'REILLY: But my point is you and Karl Rove explained your rationale. You explained it. It makes sense, at least to me. OK. You can disagree with it. The viewers can disagree with it, but why do they get so upset?

CHARLES KRAUTHAMMER: Well, some people think that I have attacked her personally. And I have, thus, given ammunition to the Democrats in running against her. . . . I was trying to argue for rationality in what is a very emotional issue. . . .

BILL O'REILLY: All right, Charles. We appreciate you being a stand-up guy. Thanks for coming on. (O'Reilly, Krauthammer, FNC [8:00] p.m., September 21, 2010)

Krauthammer went from calling the seat "lost" and O'Donnell a "weak candidate" to saying, after the audience criticized him, "I hope she wins." Karl Rove as well backtracked his initial analysis and discussed the intense criticism he had received.

BILL O'REILLY: Do you regret criticizing Christine O'Donnell in Delaware?

KARL ROVE: Yes. No, look, I wasn't criticizing. I was acting in my responsibility as a commentator and analyst for Fox. Bill, when you come on, you want me to be straight with you. (O'Reilly, Rove, FNC [8:00] p.m., September 17, 2010)

Obviously, Rove had criticized O'Donnell after her primary victory rather harshly—but after facing intense disapproval from his Fox News audience, he had to go on O'Reilly and claim he had not criticized her. Bill O'Reilly, having seen the audience's reaction to his two colleagues' comments, stayed in step with FNC's audience:

Ms. O'Donnell can be counted on to vote conservative down the line and to uphold Tea Party values, small government, lower taxes. In most years, neither candidate would have been nominated, but this year is very different, as you know. This year, the voters are throwing the bums out all over the place. And new people even with dubious backgrounds have a chance. Right now, a poll in Delaware says Coons leads O'Donnell 53–42, but that is not insurmountable for the Republican. If she hammers away at the left, far left posture of Mr. Coons, she will make inroads unless there's more stuff in her background that diverts attention. And that is the Memo. (O'Reilly, FNC [8:00] p.m., September 16, 2010)

This episode shows that news outlets respond to the feedback they receive from audiences. They collect it, analyze it, and then use it to craft future news content. O'Donnell lost the election to her Democratic opponent by seventeen percentage points—so, Krauthammer and Rove were absolutely correct in their initial analysis of her. Negative audience feedback caused them to soften those initially correct analyses and spend time explaining to the audience why their well-thought-out analyses were not in accord with their audiences' opinions. Herein lies the danger: news firms will eschew news that discomforts the audience—whether it is accurate, honest, or not. In this sense, the news no longer functions as news—it serves only to gratify audiences' political dispositions by telling audiences what makes them feel good.

An additional example comes from the 2012 Wisconsin gubernatorial recall election. MSNBC host Ed Schultz panders to his Democratic-leaning audience by refusing to acknowledge the correct election night projection made by NBC's statisticians:

ED SCHULTZ: Well, in many respects, it's to be expected, considering how much money was thrown at this race. You know, NBC is calling it for Walker. OK, I think it's awful close. There's a lot of absentee ballots yet that are still out, and it's going to be very, very close down to the wire. So, it's disappointing, I know, if this is going to be the result. (Schultz, MSNBC [9:00] p.m., June 5, 2012)

Once it was made resoundingly clear that Walker had prevailed in Wisconsin, MSNBC's audience, who did not favor the Republican's victory, needed gratification in another way. Even if the results of the Wisconsin recall election could not provide it, MSNBC was happy to provide gratification in other ways. Schultz went on the say that Walker would soon be criminally "indicted," and host Lawrence O'Donnell said that the big winner of the evening was "President Obama." As one would guess, Fox News Channel covered Walker's victory much more positively, and in line with their viewership's opinions.

New information about public opinion can drive news firms' coverage as well. Let's look at coverage of the Tea Party as it emerged in 2009–2010. The Tea Party's coverage was initially negative—particularly from MSNBC and CNN. FNC's coverage was more positive but still somewhat mixed as the movement was just getting started. Each station's audience would intuitively react to the Tea Party's emergence differently. We would expect FNC's conservative audience to be most supportive of the Tea Party, CNN's audience to be less so, and MSNBC's audience to be downright hostile. Therefore, we would expect FNC's coverage to be the most positive, CNN's to be less so, and MSNBC's to be even worse. To begin, Fox's coverage was generally positive, but slightly tepid as the movement first emerged: "Look, some of these Tea Party people are nuts. They are. They're crazy. I mean, we sent Jesse Watters down there. And he puts the number at about 10 percent that are just loons, out of their mind" (O'Reilly, FNC [8:00] p.m., February 8, 2010). CNN's coverage of the emerging movement was more skeptical than Fox's in general, and in some cases derogatory. CNN tried to portray the Tea Party as an extremist movement. Let's look at two segments.

DAVID GERGEN: Republicans are pretty much in disarray. . . . They have not yet come up with a compelling alternative, one that has gained popular recognition. So—

ANDERSON COOPER: Teabagging. They've got teabagging.

GERGEN: Well, they've got the teabagging. . . . This happens to a minority party after it's lost a couple of bad elections, but they're searching for their voice.

ANDERSON COOPER: It's hard to talk when you're teabagging. (Cooper, Gergen, CNN [8:00] p.m., April 14, 2009)

SUSAN ROESGEN: You know, Kyra, this is a party for Obama bashers. I have to say that this is not entirely representative of everybody in

America. . . . [to protester] You're here with your two-year-old and you're already in debt. Why are you here today, sir?

MAN: Because I hear a president say that he believed in what Lincoln stood for. Lincoln's primary thing was he believed that people had the right to liberty and they had the right—

ROESGEN: Sir, what does this have to do with taxes? Do you realize that you're eligible for a $400 credit? Did you know that the state of Lincoln gets $50 billion out of the stimulus? That's $50 billion for this state, sir. We'll move on over here. I think you get the general tenor of this. It's anti-government, anti-CNN, since this is highly promoted by the right wing conservative network, Fox. And since I can't really hear much more and I think this is not really family viewing, I'll toss it back to you. (Roesgen, CNN [2:00] p.m., April 15, 2009)

Oddly, Roesgen's reporting was at odds with the event; even though there were children at the Tea Party event, she termed it "not really family viewing," as if there were debauchery taking place. This shows that CNN was interested in creating a narrative of the group as more extreme than they actually were. Host Rachel Maddow from MSNBC went even more derogatory, as we would expect given MSNBC's mostly progressive audience. Her coverage fit very well with the progressive caricatures of the conservative Tea Party movement.

Teabagging. After spending weeks mailing teabags to members of Congress, conservative activists next week say they plan to hold tea parties to proverbially teabag the White House. And they don't want to teabag alone, if that's even possible. They want you to start teabagging, too. They want you to teabag Obama on Twitter. They want you to, quote, "send your teabag and teabag Obama on Facebook." They want you to teabag liberal Dems. before they teabag you. And all this nonconsensual conservative teabagging is just the start. All across America on Tax Day, Republican members of Congress are lining up to speak at teabag tea party events. Even Gov. Mark Sanford of South Carolina is getting in on the hot teabagging action. Sen. David Vitter of Louisiana, previously most famous for his self-admitted very serious sin with prostitution services—he wants to give teabagging the Senate seal of approval. He has asked the Senate to commemorate the day of anti-Obama protests in law. In terms of—now, no laughing offset or I will lose it. I'm only barely making it through this as it is. All right. Ready? In terms of media, our colleagues at Fox News are not just reporting on teabagging, they are officially promoting it. (Maddow, MSNBC [9:00] p.m., April 9, 2009)

As the Tea Party grew in size, it became known through public opinion polls. In April 2010, Gallup released a poll showing that about a third of the country identified with the Tea Party. The results also showed that the Tea Party drew its support from both conservatives and moderates, as well as from the educated and affluent.[1] This did not mesh with CNN's and MSNBC's narrative that the Tea Party was a fringe extreme movement. Fox News became even more supportive of the Tea Party and solidified its reputation as the place to get news for Tea Party members.

> BILL O'REILLY: One of the things that strikes me about the Tea Party is that it basically came about because people were getting fed up with big government. I mean, and it really caught fire fast. (O'Reilly, FNC [8:00] p.m., August 23, 2010)

MSNBC, despite the growth of the Tea Party, did not alter its coverage of the Tea Party. We would not expect it to, given that it had no incentive to do so. MSNBC's audience hardly overlapped with Tea Party membership, and the demands for gratification by its progressive audience would preclude any concessions toward the Tea Party regardless of their size. As polls showed the Tea Party gaining in size and influence, MSNBC chose not to acknowledge it.

> RACHEL MADDOW: We will bring you the really rich guys behind the Tea Party, *supposedly* grassroots tidal wave that is sweeping America. (Maddow, MSNBC [9:00] p.m., August 24, 2010)

CNN on the other hand, having been outflanked on both the ideological left and right, had to tread gingerly in case the Tea Party grew outside of the right-wing extreme and encompass parts of its audience. While it initially did not expect the movement to gain enough traction to overlap with CNN viewership, the Tea Party did grow rather rapidly, and in a way that may have threatened to cost CNN audience share. Polls showed that the Tea Party represented an audience that advertisers wanted to reach; it would not be in CNN's interest to alienate them. Many compared the Tea Party to the Ross Perot movement of the early 1990s; both movements focused on fiscal conservatism. CNN would probably not want to alienate that group of viewers, especially given that the Ross Perot movement started on CNN's *Larry King Live*. Upon learning of the Tea Party's growth, CNN pulled back their earlier criticism.

> DAVID GERGEN: There's a Gallup poll out now that's saying about 28 percent of Americans believe that they, you know, they're basically within the Tea Party overall effort, that they agree with what the Tea Party is trying to do. So, we're seeing a group that is trying to become mainstream, that's making strides in that direction. And it . . . reflects their frustration at what they feel has been media misrepresentations over a long period of time.
>
> ANDERSON COOPER: And fair enough on that, and I include myself on that probably early on. (Cooper, Gergen, CNN [8:00] p.m., April 8, 2010)

In addition to modifying his views on-air, Cooper also apologized off-air for his originally disparaging comments. Unfortunately for CNN, even though they tried to adjust quickly to the rising political tides, the damage was already done. As a partial consequence during the period 2009 to 2012, CNN rating dropped precipitously, and they currently occupy third place, out of three major cable news networks.

Conclusion

With evolving technology, news firms have found more efficient and less expensive means for tapping audience opinions. Whereas in the past, news firms had to either wait on clunky data or play guessing games, now they can chart opinions nearly spot-on. With this information, the temptation for newspeople to mold programming to follow those demands has increased. While this chapter shows but a few examples of this, the implications are widespread. In the attempt to gratify audiences' political predispositions, firms may alter programming, even the accuracy of the programming, to meet audience demands and retain viewers. Viewers demand gratification, and they will seek out news that gives it to them. News firms that do not provide it will suffer in terms of viewership and revenue. The problem for democratic governance is that gratifying news will leave audiences without the information they need to function in a democracy.

One problem with leaders, so it is often said, is that they live in a bubble cut off from those they lead. Unfortunately, the news environment has left the public in a bubble as well. Much like the bubble for leaders, the bubble for the public also insulates them with what they want to hear from what they need to hear. Just as isolated leaders are precluded from making good decisions, so are isolated citizens. But, giving consumers what they want is a successful business strategy. News outlets have a huge profit motive to gratify, and little motive to truly inform. This leaves audiences news starved and ill informed. Chapter 5 discusses the implications.

5

Where Can We Go?

Consuming Responsibly

If the public at large didn't agree with your choices, you'd be
out of business. It's a funny thing. . . . It's the appearance of
power versus the reality of power. It looks like as if you have
a lot of power over what you put on your show. But you don't.
Because if you didn't appeal to the public, if these people
don't like you—you do a marvelous job—I'm not question-
ing that. You do a marvelous job because you have found an
audience for your product.
—Milton Friedman, 1980

I opened this book with a quotation by a long-time journalist, Ted Koppel. The essay from which the quotation came expressed Koppel's dire
concerns about the influence of the market on news coverage. This closing chapter opens with the above quotation by Nobel Prize winner and
world-renowned economist Milton Friedman, who made this remark as
a guest on the *Phil Donahue Show*. As Friedman's banter with long-time
talk show host Phil Donahue indicates, although they both agree that
markets drive the media, his vantage point is far different from Koppel's.
Friedman, a strong proponent of free markets, would not be bothered by
the freedom that news firms have in chasing market demands. Koppel,
on the other hand, spent years in journalism and claims to be guided
by long-established traditional journalistic norms. Of course, we would
not expect an economist's view of the news to reflect the professed journalistic norms of the news profession, but it is instructive to see how

they each characterize a profit-driven news industry. Friedman would applaud it; Koppel warns us against it.

However, Friedman and Koppel agree on the empirics—that the media is run by markets, and audiences are necessary for programming to continue. In this sense, both make the argument that demands dictate content. As the evidence amassed in the previous chapters shows, markets do matter. Consumer demands and consumer choices drive and shape content. So, in answer to the question asked in the introduction of this work—whose news?—the evidence points to a simple answer: *ours*.

As Friedman suggests, a misperception pervades much discussion of the news media: this is that somehow news producers are hegemons who can dictate, without risk of consequence, news programming. Some argue that news firms follow their own biases or preferences for news, others that they are working in tandem with a political party or with the corporate structure. Maybe news firms are using their massive power over audiences to shape public opinion in a way that benefits them or their benefactors. These arguments ascribe to news producers a great deal of power not ascribed to producers of any other product: the power to stay in business regardless of consumer demand, and the ability to change people's opinions. Even long-standing billion-dollar corporations lose money and face bankruptcy when their products cannot amass enough sales and profits to cover costs. Polaroid is a prime example. And, while the news can affect the audience in some ways, its effects are somewhat limited, especially when consumer choice is involved.

News firm consolidation has been the norm for the past one hundred years. For example, a once-thriving market for newspapers has shrunk in recent decades. Advertisers saw greater value in reaching larger markets; newspapers unable to reach those larger audiences went out of business, or were acquired and merged. Newer technologies, such as radio, television, and internet, culled some of the newspaper herd. With more options to receive news (or, for that matter, other forms of entertainment), news outlets faced stiffer competition to draw in consumers. Some survived, like the *New York Times*; others are long gone.

Such market mechanisms are always with us, and always working. However, these mechanisms are not always readily apparent at any given moment. People can easily see the media outlets that operate prominently, and perhaps conclude that those outlets possess some form of magical staying power that makes them impervious. Unfortunately, people can't readily see the scores of media firms that have gone out of business over the decades. Even when large and long-respected news outlets cease to exist, people mourn their passing and move on, the nonexistent company much farther out of mind than their current available choices of news. Thus, at any given time, news producers might appear strong, in charge, hegemonic, and in no way hampered by such minor nuisances as public opinion, consumer demand, and free choice.

But such a vantage point ignores the growing mass of evidence that points to the power of the consumer over news content. In chapter 1, I laid out the broad strokes of how market forces affect news content. I contrasted this against other proposed explanations of news content. In short, other models explaining news content simply do not adequately account for the fact that news outlets must compete for audiences in a free capitalistic market.

There is little doubt that to explain all of news content, many perspectives have to be accounted for. But, in understanding news, we should focus on the theories and explanations that have the most explanatory power. There is little doubt that the biases of news firm owners, producers, editors, and journalists also seep into news coverage—recent evidence makes this clear. But, this only happens as the market allows. Conservative journalists will have the opportunity to reach larger audiences in "live free or die" New Hampshire than they would in socialist utopia Vermont. Many of Fox News' journalists and commentators have personal ideologies in line with their product's ideological reputation, but imagine a situation in which FNC's conservative audience disappeared to be replaced by a liberal audience. To stay employed and in business, the journalists and commentators at Fox would have to change their coverage immediately, despite their personal preferences, to meet the demands of the altered market. In this way, journalistic sincerity is greatly overstated: it doesn't matter much whether the reporters agree with the news they report; it only matters whether audiences agree with it. If they don't, they will not be in the audience for long.

Other supply-side models can offer some explanatory power as well, but with just as many pitfalls. Models of corporate and government control, respectively, may offer leverage in some instances, and evidence has been amassed in their favor (e.g. Bennett et al. 2007). But, in the long run corporate and government perspectives need an audience, and if they don't get it, news outlets favoring those perspectives will lose credibility, lose audiences, and perhaps cease to exist.

Events and circumstances drive news as well—but only very loosely. Obviously, the news would not be able to cover troop casualties in the Iraq War if the Iraq War never happened. But, there are millions of events occurring on any given day, and should a news firm need a story to meet a particular demand, it can find it. As sociologist Brian Monahan (2010:4) points out, the news we read, hear, and see is not a mirror-image reflection of reality; it is the product of a series of mostly purposeful choices:

> News is a social construction, which suggests that what audiences see as "news" (i.e., the finished product that arrives in our televisions, radios, newspapers, magazines, and computer monitors) is actually the tangible manifestation of a series of decisions made by the people—editors, producers, reporters, anchors, guest bookers, news promoters, and other media figures—who determine which events, issues, and individuals will be attended to, what resources will be allocated to their coverage, what aspects of an event or issue will be the focal point, which plotlines will be followed, which characters will be promoted, and so on. From a constructionist perspective, all news is a collection of individual news elements: facts and figures, images, eyewitness accounts, expert commentary, and the like. The differences in form and content are largely in the selection of news elements and the manner in which they are presented to the audience. Information and images become part of the news not because they are inherently important or provide an accurate reflection of objective

reality but because they have been defined as "newsworthy" by those whose job it is to identify potential news items and to transform them to appeal to the needs of both media officials and media audiences.

The "War on Terror" was a huge story from 2001 through 2008. At that point, the war took a back seat to a series of other, supposedly more important stories. Troops were still being killed, and the United States faced the same challenges it had in previous years. But somehow, news addressing the war on terror faded into the background. This change in coverage represented a purposeful choice—the public's interests had changed. Likewise, the overwhelming negativity found in our news media is not the product of a terrible and mean world. Bad things do happen, and news outlets do cover those bad events. But, the choice to report overwhelmingly negative news is the product of a series of decisions that serve both producers and customers.

In chapter 1, I argued that news firms constructed news with several demands in mind. In chapter 2, I looked specifically at how demands for information drove news firms to report certain issue areas. Using nearly forty years of data collected from the nightly network news broadcasts, I compared issue content to public concerns. The results suggested that the firms meet demands for information in many instances: they report stories that fall into the issue areas that concern the public. While on the one hand meeting demands for information can provide the audience with what it needs to know, on the other hand, it allows audiences to dictate their information environment. If audiences demand coverage of issues that are not particularly important, then journalists are abdicating their duty if they follow those demands. Audiences may simply choose not to demand information about subjects that are important and in need of attention; in these cases, should journalists ignore such stories? As Monahan suggests, someone, at some point, must decide what will be reported and what will not be reported. As models of traditional journalism suggest, journalists should have a greater say over news content than they do, and audiences should have a smaller say than they do. *Journalists are not there just to report; they are there to decide what should be reported.*

Chapter 3 began by showing how the distribution of political ideology in the public has driven the branding of the cable news market as well as the ratings successes of individual networks. The latter half of chapter 3 demonstrated how the supposedly more traditional nightly network news firms follow mass partisanship in constructing the issue agenda of the nightly news. As the public became more Republican, the networks subsequently reported more Republican-owned issues (Defense, Law & Crime). As the public become more Democratic, the networks followed by reporting more Democratic-owned issues (Civil Rights, Social Welfare, and Labor). Whereas traditional journalism would probably not allow for journalists putting their thumb to the wind and following the partisan disposition of the audience, it happens in cable, and even in the long-standing and long-respected traditional nightly news. Outlets shape the news to suit the audience's political dispositions.

Chapter 4 discussed the methods that outlets use to gather information about audiences. As it stands, news outlets are laden with built-in techniques for following audience opinions. Web-based news almost always allows for reader/viewer comments and feedback. Cable news frequently solicits opinions from its viewers. Given this, outlets can now react instantaneously to short-term fluctuations in public opinion. Their ability to react so quickly to a wide range of opinions has been a major driver of their success. With these tools, firms no longer need to wait for opinions to solidify over longer periods to react—now they have instant barometers up and running twenty-four hours a day. News reaction to shifts in opinions has been more accurate and instantaneous than has ever been possible in the past.

It is clear that news firms have the motives to shape their products to follow market demands. If they don't, they will probably go out of business. If journalists turn off audiences, or cannot attract an audience for their work, they lose their jobs. If firms cannot attract audiences, advertising dollars dry up. Outlets also have the means. Polling has been in use by media firms for decades, along with ratings reports. New technologies have allowed for even greater feedback from audiences over a range of topics. And the evidence suggests that economic motives drive firms to gather and use audience information in crafting their content, so as to meet demand. But, the purpose of this work goes beyond simply documenting the influence of audiences and markets on news content.

Just understanding the forces that influence news content can lead to better behavior by news consumers. Consider a person who walks into a used car dealership assuming the salesman will act in the consumer's interest. That person would be naive; the car salesman is well aware of his own interests, and is obliged to act on them by getting the highest price for the cheapest car. It is the salesman's job. Most people, however, are not so naive and are well aware of the car dealership's incentive structure. Informed consumers walk into the dealership expecting to want to pay less than the salesman may want them to pay. After negotiation, they may reach a price that suits both seller and buyer. In the car dealership, the feedback is direct and the incentives of all parties are clear and inherent.

With the media, all the incentives are there, just as in the used car lot. News firms have incentives to draw in audiences with their product; this is what determines their revenue and livelihood. And news consumers have incentives to negotiate for better product (one that better meets their demands), perhaps at a cheaper cost (costs in this case might be less direct, such as the amount of time and space allotted to advertising). However, these incentives are not quite as visible as in the used car lot. Most people assume the car salesperson wants to sell as many cars as possible at the highest prices possible. With the news, the motivations driving the content are more opaque. Audiences are not necessarily aware that markets and economics drive content. This leaves audiences at a disadvantage in being able to react to the news that news firms provide. If people operate, partially or wholly, under the assumption that the news reported is "the" news, then they will not be inclined to demand much better.

News firms obscure their incentive structures from news consumers, and instead attempt to convince audiences that they follow "traditional standards" or special "rules of ethical conduct." A brief perusal of any local nightly news broadcast or national news broadcast would indicate as much. Outlets advertise their product with prototypical catchphrases such as "the news you need to know," "if it is important, we cover it here," or "keeping you up to date with what matters." The message from news firms is that their content stems from journalists' independent judgments regarding what information is necessary for participants in a democratic society.

News firms do not draw in audiences with catchphrases such as "the news you want to hear," "the news that makes you feel good about what you already believe," or "the news that will draw your attention with violent, gruesome, and strange events." Unfortunately, such catchphrases would be better suited to the products and intents behind them. Oddly, there are many popular entertainment shows on television that advertise the latter—the content for such shows, in many instances, is similar to the opening salvos on local and cable broadcasts. By using deceiving marketing to put on the appearance of traditional journalism, news firms essentially "trick" consumers into thinking that the content they offer is something that performs a function that it does not.

The question then arises, How are consumers to know the quality news from the lesser quality news? If the public views journalists as generally out to bring the most important stories to light (even if those journalists might be ideologically biased in their coverage), wouldn't news coverage then, no matter its content, be viewed as the most important and necessary? What training do audiences have to decide that mundane traffic accidents and convenience store hold-ups, though tragic, are usually not the most important issues facing the community? How can audiences know that minor fluctuations in daily tracking polls are not the most important issues of the day? How can audiences come to decide that common gaffes and miscues from politicians and media personalities are not important stories? Judging by the amount of coverage given to the former representative Anthony Weiner (D-NY) virtual sex scandal, one would assume that Anthony Weiner was not one of 535 legislators, but rather someone who had real power to unilaterally affect policy. He did not. Furthermore, one would have assumed from the coverage it amassed that Weiner was using his virtual sexcapades to craft important bills that would affect our lives immeasurably. Or consider the attention paid to Senator Marco Rubio's sip out of a water bottle during the State of the Union rebuttal in 2013. This sip became more reported than any of his substantive arguments. Why would one not assume that if a story is in the news, it is important?

The news has changed much in recent decades. But, the forces driving news content have remained the same. Content has become even more sensationalistic, more poll driven, more interactive over the last few decades. News is now transmitted more ways; through phones, computers, satellite, and cable. But still, the forces that drive these changes are the same. This work shows that public demands have long influenced coverage in meaningful ways. In short, audiences probably have no idea what news would look like if it actually delivered what it advertised: the most important stories. Given this, audiences probably have a difficult time understanding the reach of markets into newsrooms, and the effects of markets in obscuring important issues from public view as a consequence.

It is difficult to blame audiences for not knowing what market-insulated news might look like. Perhaps it might look similar to the news provided by NPR or PBS, but then again, both of those stations must follow their audience's demands in seeking funding; they simply do it in different ways. If no one watched PBS or listened to NPR, no one would be there to contribute during pledge week, and there would be little political pressure for Congress to continue funding them. With this work being no exception, scholars have generally avoided explicitly stating what non-market-driven news would look like, except in generalities. This and other works are quick to point out what independent traditional journalists should not do: if they follow the vagaries of public opinion, if they aim to increase audience size first, if they account for the demographics of the intended market, then they are probably not following traditional journalistic standards.

Occasionally scholars make recommendations for improving the news. Synthesizing many such prior arguments, I will attempt later to provide a series of mechanisms for firms to maintain audiences while providing journalists with greater independent say over news content and audiences with more important and informative news.

While news consumers may not have the greatest handle on understanding the influence of markets, they have adapted to the news environment well in at least a few ways. First, news consumers have figured out how to ideologically sort themselves in the currently bifurcated media market. Given the number of choices, conservatives have flocked to Fox News, and liberals, as of 2008, have flocked to MSNBC. This phenomenon is similar with the internet: studies show that blog use is driven by political ideology—people read like-minded news and opinion (Lawrence et al. 2010). People are attracted to gratifying material; and they respond well by choosing the "correct" outlets. Second, news consumers have adapted to changing media delivery systems, and this demand has in turn created a healthy supply of news available at all hours of the day, on cable, on the internet, on the cell phone, etc. The demand for more news in more ways has created a public good—consumers now have information available to them with fewer barriers than were present only a few years ago. The willingness of consumers to move away from the once-a-night format or daily hard-copy format, often looked upon with dismay by media scholars, has driven the availability of news in ways never before imagined. There exists the infrastructure for good news to impact society; on the other hand, the overabundance of space to fill presents perverse incentive structures.

But, with this said, audiences are still kept at a disadvantage because they do not know the "good" from the "not-as-good." Some might make the argument that if people knew what was good for them, they would make better choices when it came time to choose which news to consume. Arguments in favor of government involvement in food labeling follow this track: people do not know what food is good for them and what food is bad for them. The most striking point of such an argument is that there are some foods that are generally healthier than others—caloric, fat, sugar, carbohydrate, and preservative content can all be measured and their effects on health can be assessed. So, for instance, a meal full of saturated fats should be passed over in favor of a meal with less such fats. But, with news content, the story driven by economic interests may not be distinguishable from the story stemming from a journalist's genuine independent judgment. Because the difference in the reporting may be in the motivation for the story, and not in the story itself, it may be difficult for consumers to make judgments on a story-by-story basis, the way people can judge each individual meal. Certainly, a government agency could not judge either.

So, what does this mean? Certainly, in some of the most flagrant instances, consumers can easily pick out stories that are reported purely to draw in audiences: people getting naked, animals doing strange things, etc. In these instances, it would be quite a leap to seriously suggest that these stories are the most important of the day, help society, or meet democratic ideals.

A more difficult case may occur in local televised news coverage. Generally these programs focus on car accidents, shootings, stabbings, or some other violent act or gruesome outcome. No doubt this style of coverage is market driven, but some of these stories may very well be important. For instance, if a particular intersection is the home of repeated death and injury, then the news should cover it to perhaps bring about public concern and resolution. On the other hand, if the story is not intended to bring about resolution, but instead is reported because it allows the opportunity to show graphic and grisly material, then it is likely that the story may not be that important for society. Although this may be hard to parse at times, the distinction lies in the motivation. And, in the example of traffic accidents, the style of reporting may say a lot. If those interviewed include passersby who are shocked by the accident, or if the visual shots include close-ups of police tape, chalk outlines, or smashed cars, it is likely that the outlet is interested in little more than appealing to the audience's natural demands for shocking material. If, on the other hand, the story featured interviews with traffic specialists, police, administrators, etc., or if the coverage shots included facts, figures, and relevant information, then this might indicate that the journalists were making an effort to use the event to improve the community.

In short, the ability of audiences to discern the market-driven news from the traditional journalism may be difficult, even for sophisticated news consumers. Because of this, beyond self-selecting the mode of news delivery and the political ideology of the news they prefer, audiences have not yet begun to act like good consumers of news. This is an important point, because when consumers demand a particular product, the available supply of products will morph to meet those demands. The fast-food industry provides an example of this: when salads came into fashion in the early 1980s, fast-food restaurants began installing salad bars. When chicken became viewed as a healthy alternative to burgers, restaurants began offering chicken nuggets and tenders. When french fries fell into disfavor, restaurants began offering apple slices. And when high-end coffees became all the rage, fast-food restaurants began offering lattes. In short, demand drives supply. Unfortunately, the demand for independent traditional journalism has not yet reached a mass critical enough to transform the currently poor quality of news.

In the next few sections, I will discuss what the findings of this book mean for American democracy, followed by solutions that could fix the problems caused by a demand-driven media. I will also include an oft-proposed solution to the problem of poor news quality; government intervention. I will argue that government-run solutions are likely to do more harm than good.

Public Influence and What It Means

This work argues that public demands drive substantive news content. But, so what? If news firms provide news that people want to consume, is that really so bad? If news firms have to turn a profit to stay in business, aren't we better off with news tailored to public demands rather than no news at all? What is the harm?

Many scholars have written about traditional journalism and its value to democracy. An independent media, following traditional journalistic values, can inform the public about pressing issues and seek resolution, describe alternatives available to voters, discourage wrongdoing by leaders, and educate the public so as to create a more enlightened society. These tasks are of monumental importance and are necessary in democratic society. But as chapter 1 argued, the current media environment often fails in these tasks, and study after study has alluded to the negative consequences these failures have for society.

Public opinions matter greatly in determining substantive news content. It comes as little shock that news outlets try to appeal as widely as possible with nonsubstantive aspects of news: visual displays, graphics, attractive anchors and reporters, etc. But, there is less clarity in the determinants of the substantive aspects of news. Audiences occasionally question the choices that newspeople make in constructing content, but, those questions rarely revolve around public influence. This book, and other works like it, attempt to shed light on the feedback loop between media and audience. In short, if change is not made in the near future, the harms done by a public-influenced news media will come to full fruition.

We have already experienced negative effects. Attention to historical fact first suggests that media outlets always had to make money in this country; at no point were the media ever free of the burdens of economics. If some were to refer to the days of yore when journalism was truly independent, democratic, and free of market influence, they would be viewing the past with rosy (and incorrect) hindsight. As chapters 2 and 3 point out, even outlets considered traditional news organizations have followed the vagaries of public opinion for decades. This influence has grown over time because the mechanism for using public demands to construct content is becoming more efficient.

The methods for gathering information about audiences have become less costly. Scientific public polling is one way that firms learn about the public. Accurate public polling has existed since the 1930s and '40s, but it has become increasingly less costly and therefore more frequent. Surveys over the telephone can now be automated, and surveys can be cheaply administered over the internet as well. As chapter 4 illustrated, news firms have undertaken a variety of methods for knowing the precise preferences of audiences. Market research that in the past was costly is now often free, instantaneous, and more precise. In short, news firms have gotten increasingly proficient at monitoring their target audiences. This has made it much easier for news firms to construct content with those preferences in mind. While some opinions are stable across time, new questions come along frequently and news firms may not know immediately if the audience demands coverage of those, how much, and in what way. With newer techniques of gathering opinions afforded by interactive technology, news firms can know immediately.

Given this, it is safe to assume that news firms will cater even more closely to audience demands as time goes on, as the use of current technology improves. And, as costs of delivering news and advertising decrease over time, we should also expect a more segmented media market. This is the case because, as production becomes cheaper, more producers can enter the market and compete for a slice of it. We have seen this for the last forty years: as cable lowered the barriers to entry, more and more channels have entered. And, as they have, newer channels, such as Fox News and MSNBC, have chased specific groups of people. This is especially true of internet news sources that have followed the same practices. Sites chase niche groups such as intelligent specialists, people on the left, people on the right, etc. And, this has not seemed to hamper the flow of advertising dollars. As news sources chase specific segments of the market, advertisers are better able than ever before to focus their attention on those most likely to purchase their product. For example, newer technologies allow advertisers to market their products specific to the audience's region, and even browsing history. So, the market segmentation of the news has provided advertisers with highly specific markets to saturate.

Some degree of segmentation has always been with us. Large cities have long hosted multiple newspapers and television stations, each addressing differing demands. However, the common sources of news, such the broadcast news programs, have lost considerable audience size in the last three decades. Newspapers have become less popular. And, internet sources of news vary widely, and even when they focus on similar content, consumers can pick and choose which stories to read, without much attention paid to what producers denote as the top stories. In short, the current media market allows each individual to choose his or her own news—journalists' decisions about what matters now may have less of an impact—and as a result, citizens are not exposed to the stories that are deemed most important by an independent body. Audiences are not pushed beyond their comfort zones, and there is no longer a public sphere of common content. People now choose from a variety of sources the news that most pleases them (if any), and as a result, each person is exposed to a vastly different array of information. Next-door neighbors, because of their news choices, may be living in very different worlds. This cuts the public sphere into a series of scattered pieces, and does not allow for a common discourse of events, issues, and politics.

This media segmentation is often cited as a prime cause of political polarization. Polarization can lead to policy deadlock or, when policies do pass, to extremist policy. Many studies argue that polarization is currently wide, and appears to be widening due to media coverage (e.g. Baum and Groeling 2008). Because people can self-select into their own realities, "truth" among people will vary widely, people will become more accustomed to using news mainly for purposes of gratification, and citizens will have less and less experience over time encountering information that counters their prior views. And, in terms of holding government accountable for its actions or providing serious, unbiased policy analysis, news firms will have less and less incentive to impugn politicians and policies that their particular segment of the audience favors. Does any serious observer believe MSNBC's Chris Matthews offers an unbiased critique of President Obama?

Under current trends, more and more people will hold increasingly disparate views of reality. There will probably cease to be a common content and baseline of knowledge. How can such an outcome be avoided? No doubt, criticisms of the news media are vast. But, viable solutions are few and far between. Let me briefly examine some of the more popular proposed solutions, and provide critique. Then, I will suggest solutions that will allow the market to run its course but at the same time provide a far more enriching news environment for democracy.

Potential Solutions

One solution to the problem of an audience-driven media is to have government involvement. Since the introduction of radio and television, the government has played a major role in managing competition within markets and a very minor role governing content through the FCC. The result of these policies has never been to improve the quality of news, nor have any of the provisions designed to make particular outlets fair done so. Much of the data presented in this book refers to periods under the "Fairness Doctrine," and the FCC managed licensing of outlets and content standards during the entirety of the time period from which this data was drawn. The data suggest that FCC oversight did not stop firms from following audience demands. FCC regulations over the years have stifled competition, but there is little indication that this led to better news quality; it simply shielded current competitors from market entry.

But, what if controls were imposed by the government compelling news firms to provide "better-quality" news? How could such a policy work? I would argue that it could not. Democratic media must, by their very nature, be independent. If government required reporting of certain stories, or even more generally, certain types of stories over others, journalists could no longer be independent from government. This would be worse than dependence on market demands. Perhaps the largest fear stemming from this is that criticism of government officials and policy would be easily quashed in favor of news that puts the government in a good light. At worst, the media would become a propaganda machine for the bureaucracy and for political leaders. The cure would be worse than the ailment: the current audience-driven news may not be independent from markets, but it is mostly independent from government. And, because government is likely to be the object of news coverage, and has the means to enforce its will with force, it is simply unfeasible to allow it to regulate coverage of itself.

For this reason, government control of news content is unfeasible, but what about government control of other aspects of news, such as funding? Could news operations become government funded without

WHERE CAN WE GO? ≫ 153

government interference into the actual content of news? In theory, yes, but in practice, no. Let's say for instance that government decided to fund the news media, but not interfere in its content. Given that the government would be holding the purse strings, it is difficult to imagine that influence could not be peddled or, worse, coerced from newsrooms. With funding on the line, journalists would no doubt pull or report certain stories following political pressures. This has been the case with PBS, who relies on some funding from government. When Republicans have had control of Congress, PBS faces threats of budget cuts—such proposals to cut funding are usually accompanied by complaints about the programming. PBS has had to be very mindful of the political winds in Congress. Funding for PBS became a wedge issue in the 2012 presidential election—Big Bird was repeatedly mentioned on the campaign stump. In short, an entity that controls the funding will eventually exert great influence over the content—this would not be unlike the public exercising control over content because their choice to consume drives the funding. Only in this case, the control would be from government officials rather than audiences. A further problem with government involvement in news is that with so many news outlets, it would be an impossible undertaking no matter the resources invested. Government involvement could not, and would not, solve the problem—it would probably only present greater dangers and be more odious than current arrangements.

Even more discouraging is that because news producers have chased audiences for so long, it is unlikely they would know how to move away from their current routines or what new routines might look like. To provide a guide for news outlets to improve the quality of their product, the following section provides seven minimally intrusive suggestions.

1. Limit sensationalism;
2. Provide substantive information;
3. Provide higher-quality commentators;
4. Displace politics with policy;
5. Allow less public voice;

6.   Create clearer demarcation between news and commentary;
7.   Achieve ideological parity.

These suggestions constitute attempts to improve news quality while still drawing in audiences.

First, news firms chase after audiences with sensational stories—often tragedy, scandal, violence, corruption, etc. These stories shock audiences and provide high entertainment value. But unfortunately, once the shock wears off, news firms move on to the next story without seeking resolution. There are probably reasons for this, for example, solutions take time. If the media act as watchdogs and expose a problem in or with government, then hearings, trials, policy solutions, and implementation could take years—these processes extend temporally beyond the audience's attention span. But, as a consequence, stories exposed by the news often don't find resolution, and if they do, the resolution is often not as widely discussed as the initial problem.

Firms can continue to report shocking material, but perhaps limit it only to those stories that may call for a solution or resolution. A litmus test for reporting stories (this applies most prominently to televised news) could be simple: Would the firm report the story if it could not provide a visual? Without visuals of police tape, smashed cars, chalk outlines, or naked people, reporters would probably overlook many of the stories that currently top headlines. Firms should also integrate follow-ups to stories months or even years down the road. Content could answer questions such as, Where is the story now? What has been done about it? What policies have been implemented, and what are their effects? Such follow-up stories would not only provide quality news, but they could also draw in audiences. If the story was originally attractive enough to report in the first place, then a follow-up could certainly draw on that initial interest to frame the substantive coverage of the ongoing aftermath or resolution. Many news outlets at the local and national level already do this to some degree. For example, *The O'Reilly Factor* features a segment called "Factor Follow Up" in which the current status of previous stories is reported. *The Dr. Phil Show* has done this successfully as well—many of the episodes feature updates on previous guests to see if their problems have been resolved. If Dr. Phil can draw in audiences with such a strategy, then it could work on the news.

Second, firms should allocate more time/space to the substantive stories they currently cover. News firms address important issues, but barely address their complexities because they attempt to fit the stories into short segments. For example, cable news firms address big, important issues, but they cut serious discussions down to two- or three-minute segments. It is simply impossible to have an informative discussion on a broad topic, like health care reform, in a ninety-second format. To address this, the internet could be put to better use. Firms could provide ongoing coverage of smaller facets of an issue, and meaningfully package them together online. Given that the internet provides limitless time and space, firms can now provide limitless amounts of quality information to audiences, and reap benefits from targeted online advertising. Firms do already provide complimentary coverage on many issues, but the potential has yet to be reached.

Third, firms should invite higher-quality guests onto radio and television and higher-quality sources for print. Cable news stations are perhaps the worst offender in terms of guest quality—stories focusing on highly technical policy issues are often discussed by people who have, in practice, little expertise in the policy area. Programs often invite "strategists," journalists, and campaign operatives to discuss policy; these types of guests often have little expertise in assessing actual *policy*. Such guests tend to convey ideological viewpoints more than to provide substantive information to viewers. A close look at cable news programming suggests that programming has become overrun with strategists of varying levels of expertise. As a consequence, many cable news discussions of policy focus on normative and strategy questions, rather than on anything relating to the actual language, provisions, or predicted outcomes of the legislation. Journalists as well are too often asked to provide commentary—in this role they do little better than the strategists. The reason for this is simple: journalists are not usually analysts, policy-wonks, or experts in any given field (sometimes they are, but often they are not).

Journalists are trained at reporting the news—and in many instances, not much else. Their commentary may be little more meaningful than anyone else's. Finally, campaign operatives (or, for that matter, former politicians, etc.) may have little more to offer than personal opinions. While these may occasionally supply the broader arguments, these guests often do little to justify their opinions with meaningful evidence or debate.

To address this, news firms should move away from these guests generally. Instead, firms should address policy discussions with people who have an expertise in the area and can provide reliable information. Such people do exist! Think tanks, policy groups, and academia can provide such expertise. One need not look further than C-SPAN's weekday morning programming to find a wealth of experts who can provide valuable information. Many experts are not only knowledgeable but also media savvy and can provide a pleasant news presence at the same time they provide expert information. No commentators or guests are perfect, but news firms should seek better.

Fourth, policy should displace politics. News firms have long covered politics as a strategic game where the only goal is to win rather than make good policy. This form of coverage has become so engrained in reporters that almost all campaign news focuses on polls, campaign strategy, and the horse race. This type of coverage is nearly meaningless and unfortunately, this coverage has been passed off as news for decades. Little attention is paid to the actual policies or their consequences and little substantive information is provided to consumers.

While scholars have long commented on the overwhelming prevalence and side effects of such coverage, little has been done to curb it. If anything, its amount has increased with the ever-increasing availability of polling data. It is very common to hear reports that begin with "new poll numbers out tonight" or "shocking new poll numbers." Polling data, as was feared for decades, has become news in and of itself (this is especially true during campaigns). Candidate issue positions rarely take center stage, unless they involve gaffes, controversy, or contention. More frequently, government officials and candidates are asked about strategy rather than policy. As a result, the focus of most political reporting is on strategy, which candidate is winning, and where the candidate stands in the polls, as opposed to what exactly the candidates stand for and what it would mean if their policies were implemented. Elections and policy debates have consequences; the public must know what those are in order to effectively participate. Unfortunately, much of what currently passes as political coverage does not work toward this end. Therefore, this type of coverage should be limited and replaced with more substantive policy coverage. A sample target for news firms might be to mention only one poll on a given topic per week.

Fifth, the public's voice should constitute a lower percentage of news coverage. Currently, news stations include poll results, viewer/reader letters, and audience tweets and texts as news. There is no greater evidence for the devolution of the news media than the fact that tweets from random audience members now count as news stories. This type of coverage should be the first to go in exchange for substantive policy discussions. No doubt, the media do a public good by providing a sphere for the public to discuss the issues of the day. Letters to the editor sections of newspapers have done this rather well for nearly three centuries. And, internet news articles now allow comments from readers. Such input from viewers should not be eliminated totally from all news sources, but it should not substitute as news. In mediums where space and time are more limited, such as half-hour broadcasts, viewer feedback should be eliminated entirely.

The dissemination of survey results should also be dramatically curtailed. Its absence should also allow room for more substantive coverage. Yes, poll results do serve a purpose. Representative democracy depends on representatives following the will of the people, and it is important for representatives to know public sentiment just as it is important for the public to know if discrepancies exist between public views and government policy. But, with this said, too much coverage has been devoted to poll numbers with the consequence that they have become news in and of themselves.

Sixth, news providers must provide clearer demarcations between news and non-news commentary programming. The lines have become increasingly blurred in recent decades. News has become commentary, and commentary has become news. Cable news networks are perhaps the most guilty of this, but newspapers are not far behind. Cable news networks have added an increasing amount of commentary-based programming. Examples include the *Rachel Maddow Show, The O'Reilly Factor, Hannity*, etc. These programs do provide commentary—and they say as much. But, even though these programs bill themselves as commentary or analysis programs, they backhandedly claim to be motivated by journalistic ideals to provide news. It is easy for people to view consuming these programs the same as consuming more substantive news programs. Newspapers have gone in the same direction: print commentators abound. And commentary is often used as an easy substitute for more meaningful reporting. Commentary can be fine, but it is provided far more than it should be and it is not separated starkly enough from actual news. And, the quality of the commentary is often suspect. Because they are asked to discuss a wide range of issues, commentators are not experts in many of the subjects they discuss. Paul Krugman, for example, was awarded the Nobel Prize for work in international trade—but in his column for the *New York Times*, Krugman often makes claims ranging well out of his specialization.

The seventh and final suggestion is for ideological parity. First, if they are going to provide commentary, outlets should include commentators of varying ideologies, and each should be given a fair shake. Second, journalists at any given outlet should be made to have greater ideological diversity as well. Currently, and for the past several decades, journalists' opinions have run far to the left of the general public (Goldberg 2009; Lichter et al. 1986). This does not instill trust in the public (Ladd 2012), and furthermore, the ideologically slanted newsrooms have in many instances become ideological echo chambers. Given the deep psychological character of political ideology and partisanship, it is very difficult for people to set their personal preferences aside and act in an unbiased manner. This is only made worse when newsrooms are occupied by people all of one viewpoint. A variety of viewpoints in the newsroom would force journalists to be more mindful of how their views affect their reporting. News editors, producers, upper management, and ownership should be no different. It would be difficult to have an affirmative action policy for political ideology in newsrooms and boardrooms; however, greater attention should be paid to ideological diversity.

The above seven suggestions could be implemented slowly and voluntarily over time, and in such a way as to maintain revenues as news quality improves. Readers should note as well that the suggestions above do not call for all news to become high-end and wonkish. Instead, news firms should implement fixes to limit the amount of space provided for low-quality coverage.

The next discussion focuses on broader fixes to society in general. News firms can change their products—but, demands need to change as well if higher-quality news is to be economically viable. Unfortunately, societal fixes are unlikely to come in the short term, if at all—they are expensive undertakings. But, they deserve discussion because they would benefit society in their own right. These fall into three categories: education for masses, training for journalists, and watchdogs for the media.

First, K-12 education standards must be raised. Students should leave high school education with a far greater understanding of societal issues than they do now. First, students must get a more stringent education in basic skills: reading, writing, arithmetic, and scientific reasoning. This should create a knowledgeable citizenry who can competently follow high-level news coverage. Second, students in the K-12 levels should receive more substantive exposure to political science, public policy, philosophy, law, sociology, communication, and psychology. These subjects are generally given short shrift until college (and not everyone attends college), but they are necessary for good democratic decision making.

Second, journalists should have better training. Journalists should have expertise in the areas they cover, but many do not. Journalists are often asked to report and comment on a wide variety of topics that stretch the bounds of their knowledge. A simple fix might encourage future newspeople to double major in both journalism and, say, political science, economics, criminology, etc., while in college. Journalists perhaps should be encouraged to get master's degrees not in journalism but in the substantive area they cover as well. In addition to having a substantive knowledge base, journalists should have a broad understanding of science, statistics, economic data, polling data, etc. Those who transmit information should understand the information themselves.

Third, media watchdog groups should become more prevalent. News firms should face great scrutiny, just as politicians should face great scrutiny. Media watchdogs have recently sprung up, and have done a good job of watching for media bias. Unfortunately, these groups, such as Media Research Center and Media Matters, do this from their own biased ideological viewpoints. Recently, groups such as PolitFact have gained notoriety as supposedly unbiased arbiters of statements politicians make about important policy issues. Fact-checking has entered public discussions, particularly during campaign seasons. What journalism requires is perhaps a hybrid of these two types of groups—a group(s) that can monitor news content and grade it on the basis of several dimensions of quality, accuracy, unbiasedness, etc. This could act like a *Consumer Reports* for media outlets. This way, news consumers can know what they are getting.

Conclusion

News institutions are important parts of democratic societies. They can make democracy better, or they can make it worse. The news currently provides some of what democracy requires of it—but not all. Some of the news that firms do supply actually hinders democracy—perhaps to the point of negating any gains. News firms can take painless steps to improve their coverage so that it becomes more beneficial to democratic citizens. And society can take steps to better produce democratic citizens. But in the long term, the news reflects society—the uneducated, the uninterested, and the hyper-ideological receive exactly what they ask for: unsophisticated, nonrelevant, and biased news. Until society invests in making the long-term systematic changes that will forever alter society in such a way that demands change, it is unlikely that massive changes will ever truly take hold.

The media have been targeted with a great deal of criticism over the years. Some of it is deserved. Some of it is not. But, when we criticize the news, who are we really criticizing? Public demands drive coverage, and whether critics want to admit it or not, the audience is more to blame than the producers. Until our demands change, we can probably expect more of the same.

NOTES

NOTES TO CHAPTER 1

1. Company 2010; Emily Guskin and Tom Rosenstiel, "Economics" section of "The State of the News Media 2012: An Annual Report on American Journalism," *Pew Research Center's Project for Excellence in Journalism*, available at http://stateofthe-media.org/2012/network-news-the-pace-of-change-accelerates/network-by-the-numbers/#economics, last accessed May 1, 2013.

2. The broadcast media does face some regulation from the FCC; but even with this, the FCC does not regulate the content of news programming in any substantial way.

3. These two categories are often exclusive, but not necessarily: a story could both serve the public good and draw in large audiences.

4. I do note, however, that in some circumstances, soft news programs can reach news-averse audiences (Baum 2002).

5. According to LexisNexis.

6. According to LexisNexis.

7. "Media Bias Basics: How the Media Vote," *Media Research Center*, available at http://archive.mrc.org/biasbasics/biasbasics3.asp#TV%20and%20Newspaper%20 Journalists, last accessed May 1, 2013.

8. Daniel Newshauser, 2012, "Miami Attack May Push Ban on Bath Salts," available at http://www.rollcall.com/issues/57_144/Miami-Attack-May-Push-Action-on-Bath-Salts-Ban-215013-1.html, last accessed June 10, 2013.

NOTES TO CHAPTER 2

1. I note here that having public news sources as a comparison would be advantageous. However, transcripts for PBS and NPR are not available for a substantial portion of the time frame under study.

2. This archive is used frequently; recent examples include Schneider and Jacoby (2005), Eshbaugh-Soha and Peake (2005), and Damore (2005). For more on the Vanderbilt Archive, see Lynch (1996).

3. Two coders each coded half of the data. The two coders were not aware of the hypotheses being tested. The coders read the abstracts and placed them into one

of the categories. To ensure reliability, each coder was instructed to recode a random sample of the other's stories. This provided 1,378 recoded stories; the coders agreed on 94 percent. I calculated Krippendorff's Alpha for the whole of the recoded stories, and between similar categories of stories—this led to coefficients of an acceptable range, above .8.

4. The first quarter in the study is truncated as Vanderbilt did not begin archiving until the middle of the third quarter, 1968. This provides a range of 234 to 398 stories per quarter and a standard deviation of thirteen stories per quarter. Excluding that first quarter leads to a range of 368 to 396. I include this first observation in later analyses and address it by employing percentages.

5. The Policy Agendas project has compiled this time-series by averaging responses to several polls during each quarter. This data is only available through 2007; therefore the analysis runs 1968 through 2007. Networks attempt to attract the audience demographics most desired by their advertisers; this segment, or the target audience, is not necessarily equivalent to the population represented in public opinion samples. However, the 25- to 54-year-old target audience generally sought after by advertisers is not a far cry from the Gallup national samples (Ozanich and Wirth 2004).

6. This is in opposition to designs that include multiples sources of news and publics. For instance, Gentzkow and Shapiro (2006) use multiple local news broadcasts and cross-sectional measures of localized public opinion. Pollock and colleagues (1998, 1999, 2004, 2006a, 2005), as well as Branton and Dunaway (2009), employ newspaper coverage from multiple local markets and compare coverage to local characteristics such as income, partisan affiliation, and religious affiliation.

7. More detailed results of the statistical tests may be obtained from the author.

NOTES TO CHAPTER 3

1. Issue ownership is nuanced and may vary over time (Walgrave et al. 2009; Brasher 2009; Pope and Woon 2009; Sides 2006:413–14; Holian 2004; Petrocik 1996). Party reputations are long-standing, but not impervious to change in response to conditions, the arrival of new issues, and party performance. With this said, previous literature shows that ownership of these five issues is fairly stable during the years 1968–2004 (Puglisi 2011); the public consistently identifies these as "owned." Accordingly, the analysis here will speak to those years specifically.

2. I initially operationalize these as the proportion of those identifying Democratic-owned issues to those identifying Republican-owned issues; however, I parse these out in subsequent analyses.

3. Operationalizing these separately leads to similar results.

4. Besides the variables mentioned here, I tested a broad range of others. None predicted the news agenda very well.

5. Impulse response functions are available upon request from the author.

6. One important concept not tested so far in this chapter is the role that bias of newspeople plays. If newspeople's partisanship shifts the same way over time as

the population's partisanship, then the results of this chapter probably speak to a supply-side model of news content rather than to the demand-side model so far argued for. The results found here would simply indicate that reporters' partisanship, rather than the mass public's partisanship, affects news content. To examine this, it would be ideal to have an uninterrupted time-series of broadcast newspeople's partisanship to compare to the time-series of mass partisanship. If newspeople's and the public's partisanship fluctuated the same way, then we would cast doubt on the ability of the public to affect the reporting of party-owned issues through their partisanship. Unfortunately, such a time-series of news personnel partisanship does not exist. With this said, sporadic polls have asked journalists their partisan preferences. Using these, I constructed an interrupted time-series of newspeople's partisanship and compared it to macropartisanship. This comparison suggests that newspeople's partisanship does not follow the same trajectory as the public's; this is probably because newspeople are highly informed elites with well-formed political opinions. Thus, the evidence suggests that the *public's* changing partisanship affects news content.

7. This is partially due to combining Republican- and Democratic-owned issues in this way. When they are separated, we find results similar to those found in chapter 2.

NOTES TO CHAPTER 4

1. Lydia Saad, "Tea Partiers Are Fairly Mainstream in Their Demographics," *Gallup Politics*, April 5, 2010, available at http://www.gallup.com/poll/127181/tea-partiers-fairly-mainstream-demographics.aspx, last accessed May 1, 2013.

REFERENCES

Abramson, Paul R. 1976. "Generational Change and the Decline of Party Identification in America: 1952–1974." *American Political Science Review* 70: 469–78.

Allen, Craig. 1995. "Priorities of General Managers and News Directors in Anchor Hiring." *Journal of Media Economics* 8: 111–24.

Allport, Floyd H., and Lepkin Milton. 1943. "Building War Morale with News-Headlines." *Public Opinion Quarterly* 7: 211–21.

Alterman, Eric. 2003. *What Liberal Media? The Truth about Bias and the News.* New York: Basic Books.

Althaus, Scott L. 2003. *Collective Preferences in Democratic Politics: Opinion Surveys and the Will of the People.* Cambridge: Cambridge University Press.

Althaus, Scott L., Anne M. Cizmar, and James Gimpel. 2009. "Media Supply, Audience Demand, and the Geography of News Consumption in the United States." *Political Communication* 26: 249–77.

Althaus, Scott L., Jill Edy, and Patricia Phalen. 2002. "Using the Vanderbilt Television Abstracts to Track Broadcast News Content: Possibilities and Pitfalls." *Journal of Broadcasting & Electronic Media* 46: 473–92.

Anders, Charlie Jane. 2010. "How the Nielson TV Ratings Work—and What Could Replace Them." *Io9 Backgrounder,* Sept. 17. Available online.

Arceneaux, Kevin, and Martin Johnson. 2010. "Does Media Fragmentation Produce Mass Polarization? Selective Exposure and a New Era of Minimal Effects." Paper presented at APSA 2010 Annual Meeting. Available at SSRN: http://ssrn.com/abstract=1642723.

Arceneaux, Kevin, Martin Johnson, and Chad Murphy. 2012. "Polarized Political Communication, Oppositional Media Hostility, and Selective Exposure." *Journal of Politics* 74(1): 174–86.

Arnold, Douglas R. 2004. *Congress, the Press, and Political Accountability.* Princeton, NJ: Princeton University Press.

Atkin, Charles K., and Walter Gantz. 1978. "Television News and Political Socialization." *Public Opinion Quarterly* 42: 183–98.

Atkin, Charles K., and James Gaudino. 1984. "The Impact of Polling on the Mass Media." *Annals of the American Academy of Political and Social Science* 472: 119–28.

Bae, Hyuhn-Bae. 1999. "Product Differentiation in Cable Programming: The Case in the Cable National All-News Networks." *Journal of Media Economics* 12: 265–77.

Bagdikian, Ben J. 2004. *The New Media Monopoly*. Boston: Beacon.

Baker, C. Edwin. 2002. "Media, Markets, and Democracy." In *Communication, Society, and Politics*, eds. W. Lance Bennett and Robert M. Entman. Cambridge: Cambridge University Press.

Barabas, Jason, and Jennifer Jerit. 2009. "Estimating the Causal Effects of Media Coverage on Policy-Specific Knowledge." *American Journal of Political Science* 53: 73–89.

Barker, David, and Adam Lawrence. 2004. "Media Favoritism and Presidential Primaries: Reviving the Direct Effects Model." Paper presented at the Western Political Science Association, Portland, OR, March 11.

Baron, David P. 2006. "Persistent Media Bias." *Journal of Public Economics* 90: 1–36.

Bartels, Larry M. 1991. "Instrumental and 'Quasi-Instrumental' Variables." *American Journal of Political Science* 35: 777–800.

———. 1993. "Messages Received: The Political Impact of Media Exposure." *American Political Science Review* 87: 267–85.

Baum, Mathew A. 2002. "Sex, Lies, and War: How Soft News Brings Foreign Policy to the Inattentive Public." *American Political Science Review* 96: 91–109.

———. 2003. "Soft News and Political Knowledge: Evidence of Absence or Absence of Evidence?" *Political Communication* 20: 173–90.

Baum, Matthew A., and Tim Groeling. 2008. "New Media and the Polarization of American Political Discourse." *Political Communication* 25: 345–65.

Baumgartner, Frank, and Bryan Jones. 2006. "Policy Agendas Project: Topics Codebook." *Policy Agendas Project*. Available at http://www.policyagendas.org/page/topic-codebook. Last accessed April 25, 2013.

Baumgartner, Frank, Bryan Jones, and B. L. Leech. 1997a. "Media Attention and Congressional Agendas." In *Do the Media Govern? Politicians, Voters, and Reporters in America*, eds. Shanto Iyengar and R. Reeves. Thousand Oaks, CA: Sage. 349–63.

Baumgartner, Frank, Bryan Jones, and James L. True. 1997b. "Does Incrementalism Stem from Political Consensus or from Institutional Gridlock?" *American Journal of Political Science* 41 (Oct. 1997): 1319–39.

Behr, Roy L., and Shanto Iyengar. 1985. "Television News, Real-World Cues, and Changes in the Public Agenda." *Public Opinion Quarterly* 49: 38–57.

Belt, Todd L., and Marion R. Just. 2008. "The Local News Story: Is Quality a Choice?" *Political Communication* 25: 194–215.

Bennett, Stephen E. 1997. "Why Young Americans Hate Politics, and What We Should Do about It." *Political Science and Politics* 30: 47–53.

Bennett, W. Lance. 2009. *News: The Politics of Illusion*. New York: Pearson.

Bennett, W. Lance, Regina G. Lawrence, and Steven Livingston. 2007. *When the Press Fails: Political Power and the News Media from Iraq to Katrina*. Chicago: Univeristy of Chicago Press.

Bennett, W. Lance, and William Serrin. 2005. "The Watchdog Role." In *The Press*, eds. Geneva Overholser and Kathleen Hall Jamieson. Oxford: Oxford University Press.

Berelson, Bernard, Paul Lazarsfeld, and William McPhee. 1954. *Voting: A Study of Opinion Formation in a Presidential Campaign*. Chicago: University of Chicago Press.

Bineham, Jeffery L. 1988. "A Historical Account of the Hypodermic Model in Mass Communication." *Communication Monographs* 55: 230–46.

Birkland, Thomas A. 1998. "Focusing Events, Mobilization, and Agenda Setting." *Journal of Public Policy* 18: 53–74.

Blood, D. 1996. "Economic Headline News, Consumer Sentiment, Presidential Popularity, and the State of the Economy: A Study of Their Dynamic Relationship, 1980–1993." Ph.D. dissertation, University of Connecticut, Storrs.

Blood, Deborah J., and Peter C. B. Phillips. 1997. "Economic Headline News on the Agenda: New Approaches to Understanding Causes and Effects." In *Communication and Democracy*, eds. Maxwell E. McCombs, Donald L. Shaw, and David H. Weaver. Mahwah, NJ: Erlbaum.

Bovitz, Gregory L., James N. Druckman, and Arthur Lupia. 2002. "When Can a News Organization Lead Public Opinion? Ideology versus Market Forces in Decisions to Make News " *Public Choice* 113: 127–55.

Box-Steffensmeier, Janet M., and Suzanna DeBoef. 2001. "Macropartisanship and Macroideology in the Sophisticated Electorate." *Journal of Politics* 63: 232–48.

Brandt, Patrick T., and John T. Williams. 2007. *Multiple Time Series Models: Quantitative Applications in the Social Science*. Thousand Oaks, CA: Sage.

Branton, Regina, and Johanna Dunaway. 2009. "Spatial Proximity to the U.S.–Mexico Border and Local News Coverage of Immigration Issues." *Political Research Quarterly* 62(2): 289–302.

Brasher, Holly. 2009. "The Dynamic Character of Political Party Evaluations." *Party Politics* 15: 69–92.

Brock, David, and Ari Rabin-Hayt. 2012. *The Fox Effect: How Roger Ailes Turned a Network into a Propaganda Machine*. New York: Anchor.

Budge, Ian, and Dennis Farlie. 1983. "Party Competition: Selective Emphasis or Direct Confrontation? An Alternative View with Data." In *Western European Party Systems*, eds. Hans Daadler and Peter Mair. Beverly Hills, CA: Sage.

Burgoon, Judee K., Michael Burgoon, and Charles K. Atkin. *The World of the Working Journalist*. Newspaper Advertising Bureau, 1982.

Campbell, Angus, Philip Converse, Warren Miller, and Donald E. Stokes. 1960. *The American Voter*. Unabridged edition. Chicago: University of Chicago Press.

———. 1966. *Elections and the Political Order*. New York: Wiley.

Campbell, Angus, Gerald Gurin, and Warren Miller. 1954. *The Voter Decides*. Evanston, IL: Row, Peterson.

Caplan, Bryan. 2008. *The Myth of the Rational Voter: Why Democracies Choose Bad Policies*. Princeton, NJ: Princeton University Press.

Cappella, Joseph N., and Kathleen Hall Jamieson. 1996. "News Frames, Political Cynicism, and Media Cynicism." *Annals of the American Academy of Political and Social Science* 546: 71–84.

Cardwell, Michael. 2005. "Media Bias and Media Markets." Paper presented at the Annual Meeting of the American Political Science Association, Washington DC.

Chaffee, S. H., and Stacey Frank. 1996. "How Americans Get Political Information: Print versus Broadcast News." *Annals of the American Academy of Political and Social Science* 546: 48–58.

Chaffee, S. H., and J. L. Hochheimer. 1985. "The Beginnings of Political Communication Research in the United States: Origins of the 'Limited Effects' Model." In *The Media Revolution in America and in Western Europe*, eds. Everett M. Rogers and F. Balle. Norwood, NJ: Ablex. 267–96.

Chomsky, Daniel. 1999. "The Mechanisms of Management Control at the *New York Times*." *Media, Culture & Society* 21: 579–99.

———. 2006. "An Interested Reader: Measuring Ownership Control at the *New York Times*." *Critical Studies in Media Communication* 23: 1–18.

Chomsky, Noam. 1989. *Necessary Illusions*. Boston: South End Press.

Chyi, Hsiang Iris, and Maxwell McCombs. 2004. "Media Salience and the Process of Framing: Coverage of the Columbine School Shootings." *Journalism & Mass Communication Quarterly* 81: 22–35.

"CNN Tries 'Diverse' Approach." 2011. *New York Post*, April 13, 2011.

Cohen, B. 1963. *The Press and Foreign Policy*. Princeton, NJ: Princeton University Press.

Collins, Anthony. 2001. *Words of Fire: Independent Journalists Who Challenge Dictators, Drug Lords, and Other Enemies of a Free Press*. New York: New York University Press.

Collins, Scott. 2004. *Crazy like a Fox: The Inside Story of How Fox News Beat CNN*. New York: Portfolio.

Company, The New York Times. 2010. "2010 Form 10-K." Ed. United States Securities and Exchange Commission.

Conway, M. Margeret, David Ahern, and Miel L. Wyckoff. 1981. "The Mass Media and Changes in Adolescents' Political Knowledge during an Election Cycle." *Political Behavior* 3: 69–80.

Cook, Fay L., and W. G. Skogan. 1991. "Convergent and Divergent Voice Models of the Rise and Fall of Policy Issues." In *Agenda Setting: Readings on Media, Public Opinion, and Policy Making*, David L. Protess and Maxwell McCombs. Hillsdale, NJ: Erlbaum. 189–205.

Covert, Tawnya J. Adkins, and Philo C. Wasburn. 2007. "Measuring Media Bias: A Content Analysis of *Time* and *Newsweek* Coverage of Domestic Social Issues, 1975–2000." *Social Science Quarterly* 88: 690–706.

Craig, Stephen C., and Stephen Earl Bennett, eds. 1997. *After the Boom: The Politics of Generation X*. New York: Rowman & Littlefield.

Dagnes, Alison. 2010. *Politics on Demand: The Effects of 24-Hour News on American Politics*. Santa Barbara, CA: Praeger.

D'Alessio, D., and M. Allen. 2000. "Media Bias in Presidential Elections: A Meta-Analysis." *Journal of Communication* 50: 133–56.

Damore, David F. 2005. "Issue Convergence in Presidential Campaigns." *Political Behavior* 27: 71–97.

Dean, Tim. 2010. "Evolved Fear of Sharks Prompts Front Page News." *Ockham's Beard: Philosophical Adventures in a Complex World.* Available at http://ockhamsbeard. wordpress.com/?s=evolved+fear+of+sharks. Last accessed April 23, 2012.

Della Vigna, Stefano, and Ethan Kaplan. 2007. "The Fox News Effect: Media Bias and Voting." *Quarterly Journal of Economics* 122: 1187–234.

Druckman, James N., Jordan Fein, and Thomas J. Leeper. 2012. "A Source of Bias in Public Opinion Stability." *American Political Science Review* 106: 430–54.

Druckman, James N., and Michael Parkin. 2004. "Media Bias and Its Effect on Voters." Paper presented at the Annual Meeting of the Midwest Political Science Association, Chicago, IL.

Dunaway, Johanna. 2008. "Markets, Ownership, and the Quality of Campaign News Coverage." *Journal of Politics* 70: 1193–202.

———. 2012. "Media Ownership and Story Tone in Campaign News Coverage." *American Politics Research,* published online 8 August. Available at http://apr. sagepub.com/content/early/2012/07/25/1532673X12454564. Last accessed April 23, 2013.

Eagly, Alice H., and Shelley Chaiken. 1993. *The Psychology of Attitudes.* Fort Worth, TX: Harcourt Brace Jovanovich.

Edwards, George C., and B. Dan Wood. 1999. "Who Influences Whom? The President, Congress, and the Media." *American Political Science Review* 93: 327–44.

Eggers, Andrew, and Jens Hainmuller. 2011. "Capitol Losses: The Mediocre Performance of Congressional Stock Portfolios, 2004–2008." *MIT Political Science Department Research Paper Series,* no. 2011-5. Available at http://www.mit.edu/~jhainm/ Paper/Eggmueller_CapitolLosses.pdf: MIT. Last accessed April 23, 2013.

Enda, Jodi. 2011. "Retreating from the World." *American Journalism Review,* December/January. Available at http://www.ajr.org/article.asp?id=4985. Last accessed April 23, 2013.

Endersby, James W., and Ekaterina Ognianova. 1997. "A Spatial Model of Ideology and Political Communication." *Harvard International Journal of Press/Politics* 2: 23–39.

Entman, Robert M. 1989a. *Democracy without Citizens: Media and the Decay of American Politics.* Oxford: Oxford University Press.

———. 1989b. "How the Media Affect What People Think: An Information Processing Approach." *Journal of Politics* 51: 347–70.

———. 2005. "The Nature and Sources of News." In *The Press,* eds. Geneva Overholser and Kathleen Hall Jamieson. Oxford: Oxford University Press.

Entman, Robert M., and Steven S. Wildman. 1992. "Reconciling Economic and Non-Economic Perspectives on Media Policy: Transcending the 'Marketplace of Ideas.'" *Journal of Communication* 42: 5–19.

Epstein, E. J. 1981. "The Selection of Reality." In *What's News: The Media in American Society,* ed. E. Abel. New Brunswick, NJ: Institute for Contemporary Studies.

Erbring, Lutz, Edie N. Goldenberg, and Arthur H. Miller. 1980. "Front-Page News and Real-World Cues: A New Look at Agenda Setting by the Media." *American Journal of Political Science* 24: 16–49.

Erfle, Stephen, Henry McMillan, and Bernard Grofman. 1990. "Regulation Via Threats: Politics, Media Coverage, and Oil Pricing Decisions." *Public Opinion Quarterly* 54: 48–63.

Erikson, Robert S., Michael MacKuen, and James Stimson. 1998. "What Moves Macropartisanship? A Response to Green, Palmquist, and Schickler." *American Political Science Review* 92: 901–12.

Erikson, Robert S., and Kent L. Tedin. 2005. *American Public Opinion: Its Origins, Content, and Impact.* 7th ed. New York: Pearson Longman.

Eshbaugh-Soha, Matthew, and Jeffrey S. Peake. 2005. "Presidents and the Economic Agenda." *Political Research Quarterly* 58: 127–38.

Eveland, William P., Andrew Hayes, Dhavan V. Shah, and Nojin Kwak. 2005. "Understanding the Relationship between Communication and Political Knowledge: A Model Comparison Approach Using Panel Data " *Political Communication* 22: 423–46.

Eveland, William P., Krisztina Marton, and Mihye Seo. 2004. "Moving Beyond 'Just the Facts.'" *Communication Research* 31: 82–108.

Fallows, James. 1997. *Breaking the News: How the Media Undermine American Democracy.* New York: Vintage.

Farnsworth, Stephen J., and S. Robert Lichter. 2010. *The Nightly News Nightmare: Media Coverage of U.S. Presidential Elections, 1988–2008.* 3rd ed. Lanham, MD: Rowman & Littlefield.

——. 2011. "Network Television's Coverage of the 2008 Presidential Election." *American Behavioral Scientist* 55: 354–70.

Fengler, Susanne, and Stephan Russ-Mohl. 2008. "The Crumbling Wall: Towards an Economic Theory of Journalism." *Kyklos* 61: 520–42.

Ferguson, Douglas A. 2004. "The Broadcast Television Networks." In *Media Economics: Theory and Practice*, eds. Alison Alexander, James Owers, Rod Carveth, C. Ann Hollifield, and Albert N. Greco, 3rd ed. Mahwah, NJ: Erlbaum.

Fiorina, Morris P. 1981. *Retrospective Voting in American National Elections.* New Haven, CT: Yale University Press.

Forgette, Richard, and Jonathan S. Morris. 2006. "High-Conflict Television News and Public Opinion." *Political Research Quarterly* 59: 447–56.

Francke, Warren. 1995. "The Evolving Watchdog: The Media's Role in Government Ethics." *Annals of the American Academy of Political and Social Science* 537: 109–21.

Franken, Al. 2003. *Lies (and the Lying Liars Who Tell Them): A Fair and Balanced Look at the Right.* New York: Dutton.

Freeman, John R., John T. Williams, and Tse-min Lin. 1989. "Vector Autoregression and the Study of Politics." *American Journal of Political Science* 33: 842–77.

Funkhouser, G. Ray. 1973. "The Issues of the Sixties: An Exploratory Study in the Dynamics of Public Opinion." *Public Opinion Quarterly* 37: 62–75.

Gans, Herbert J. 1979. *Deciding What's News*. New York: Random House.

Garramone, Gina M., and Charles K. Atkin. 1986. "Mass Communication and Political Socialization: Specifying the Effects." *Public Opinion Quarterly* 50: 76–86.

Geer, John. 2004. *Public Opinion and Polling around the World: A Historical Encyclopedia*. Santa Barbara, CA: ABC-CLIO.

Gentzkow, Matthew, and Jesse Shapiro. 2006. "Media Bias and Reputation." *Journal of Political Economy* 114: 280–316.

———. 2010. "What Drives Media Slant? Evidence from U.S. Daily Newspapers." *Econometrica* 78: 35–71.

Gerber, Alan, Dean Karlan, and Daniel Bergan. 2006. "Does the Media Matter? A Field Experiment Measuring the Effect of Newspapers on Voting Behavior and Political Opinions." *American Economic Journal: Applied Economics* 1(2): 35–52.

Gilens, Martin. 2001. "Political Ignorance and Collective Policy Preferences." *American Political Science Review* 95: 379–96.

Giles, David. 2003. *Media Psychology*. Mahwah, NJ: Erlbaum.

Gilliam, Franklin D., Shanto Iyengar, Adam Simon, and Oliver Wright. 1996. "Crime in Black and White." *Harvard International Journal of Press/Politics* 1: 6–23.

Goidel, Robert K., and Ronald E. Langley. 1995. "Media Coverage of the Economy and Aggregate Economic Evaluations: Uncovering Evidence of Indirect Media Effects." *Political Research Quarterly* 48: 313–28.

Goldberg, Bernard. 2002. *Bias: A CBS Insider Exposes How the Media Distort the News*. Washington, DC: Regnery.

———. 2009. *A Slobbering Love Affair: The True (and Pathetic) Story of the Torrid Romance between Barack Obama and the Mainstream Media*. New York: Regnery.

Gollin, Albert E. 1980. "Exploring the Liaison between Polling and the Press." *Public Opinion Quarterly* 44: 445–61.

Gonzalez, George A. 2005a. *The Politics of Air Pollution: Urban Growth, Ecological Modernization, and Symbolic Inclusion*. Albany: State University of New York Press.

———. 2005b. "Urban Sprawl, Global Warming, and the Limits of Ecological Modernisation." *Environmental Politics* 14: 344–62.

Grabe, Maria Elizabeth, Shuhua Zhou, and Brooke Barnett. 2001. "Explicating Sensationalism in Television News: Content and the Bells and Whistles of Form." *Journal of Broadcasting & Electronic Media* 45: 635–55.

Graber, Doris. 1986. "Press Freedom and the General Welfare." *Political Science Quarterly* 101: 257–75.

———. 1994. "Why Voters Fail Information Tests: Can the Hurdles Be Overcome?" *Political Communication* 11: 331–46.

Granger, C. W. J. 1969. "Investigating Causal Relations by Econommetric Models and Cress Spectral Techniques." *Econometrica* 37: 424–38.

Groseclose, Tim. 2011. *Left Turn: How Liberal Media Bias Distorts the American Mind*. New York: St. Martin's.

Groseclose, Tim, and Jeff Milyo. 2005. "A Measure of Media Bias." *Quarterly Journal of Economics* 120: 1191–237.

Hamilton, James T. 1998. *Channeling Violence: The Economic Market for Violent Television Programming.* Princeton, NJ: Princeton University Press.

———. 2004. *All the News That's Fit to Sell: How the Market Transforms Information into News.* Princeton, NJ: Princeton University Press.

———. 2005. "The Market and the Media." In *The Press*, eds. Geneva Overholser and Kathleen Hall Jamieson. Oxford: Oxford University Press. 351–71.

Haskins, Jack B. 1981. "The Trouble with Bad News." *Newspaper Research Journal* 2: 3–16.

Hayes, Danny. 2005. "How Issue Ownership Influences the News." Paper presented at the Annual Meeting of the American Political Science Association, Washington, DC.

———. 2008. "Party Reputations, Journalistic Expectations: How Issue Ownership Influences Election News." *Political Communication* 25: 377–400.

Heath, Chip. 1996. "Do People Prefer to Pass Along Good or Bad News? Valence and Relevance of News as Predictors of Transmission Propensity." *Organizational Behavior and Human Decision Processes* 68: 79–94.

Herman, Edward S., and Noam Chomsky. 1988. *Manufacturing Consent: The Political Economy of the Mass Media.* New York: Pantheon.

Hetherington, Marc J. 1996. "The Media's Role in Forming Voters' National Economic Evaluations in 1992." *American Journal of Political Science* 40: 372–95.

Hillstorm, Laurie Collier. 2006. *Television in American Society Reference Library: Almanac.* New York: UXL Publishers.

Holian, David B. 2004. "He's Stealing My Issues! Clinton's Crime Rhetoric and the Dynamics of Issue Ownership." *Political Behavior* 26: 95–124.

Hopkins, Daniel J., and Jonathan M. Ladd. 2012. "The Reinforcing Effects of Fox News." Available at http://people.iq.harvard.edu/~dhopkins/FoxPersuasion021212.pdf.

Iyengar, Shanto, and Kyu S. Hahn. 2009. "Red Media, Blue Media: Evidence of Ideological Selectivity in Media Use." *Journal of Communication* 59: 19–39.

Iyengar, Shanto, Kyu S. Hahn, Jon A. Krosnick, and John Walker. 2008. "Selective Exposure to Campaign Communication: The Role of Anticipated Agreement and Issue Public Membership." *Journal of Politics* 70: 186–200.

Iyengar, Shanto, Helmut Norpoth, and Kyu S. Hahn. 2004. "Consumer Demand for Election News: The Horserace Sells." *Journal of Politics* 66: 157–75.

Iyengar, Shanto, Mark D. Peters, and Donald R. Kinder. 1982. "Experimental Demonstrations of the 'Not-So-Minimal' Consequences of Television News Programs." *American Political Science Review* 76: 848–58.

Iyengar, Shanto, and Adam Simon. 1993. "News Coverage of the Gulf Crisis and Public Opinion." *Communication Research* 20: 365–83.

Jerit, Jennifer, Jason Barabas, and Toby Bolsen. 2006. "Citizens, Knowledge, and the Information Environment." *American Journal of Political Science* 50: 266–82.

Johnson, Roger N. 1996. "Bad News Revisited: The Portrayal of Violence, Conflict, and Suffering on Television News." *Peace and Conflict: Journal of Peace Psychology* 2: 201–16.

Johnston, Wendy M., and Graham C. L. Davey. 1997. "The Psychological Impact of Negative TV News Bulletins: The Catastrophizing of Personal Worries." *British Journal of Psychology* 88: 85–91.

Jordan, Donald L., and Benjamin I. Page. 1992. "Shaping Foreign Policy Opinions: The Role of TV News." *Journal of Conflict Resolution* 36: 227–41.

Joslyn, Mark R., and Steve Ceccoli. 1996. "Attentiveness to Television News and Opinion Change in the Fall 1992 Presidential Campaign." *Political Behavior* 18: 141–70.

Journalists. 2010. "2010 Pages: State of the Media." *State of the News Media*. Available at http://stateofthemedia.org/2010. Last accessed June 10, 2013.

Journalists, Society of Professional. 1996. "SPJ Code of Ethics." *Society of Professional Journalists*. Available at http://www.spj.org/ethicscode.asp. Last accessed April 23, 2013.

Joyella, Mark. 2010. "Huh? CNN Spins Worst Ratings in Years: '10 Million More Viewers Than Fox News.'" Available at http://www.mediaite.com/tv/huh-facing-worst-ratings-in-years-cnn-spins-numbers-%E2%80%9C10-million-more-viewers-than-fox-news%E2%80%9D. Last accessed June 12, 2012.

Katz, E., J. G. Blumler, and M. Gurevitch. 1974. "Utilization of Mass Communication by the Individual." In *The Uses of Mass Communications: Current Perspectives on Gratifications Research*, eds. J. G. Blumler and E. Katz. Beverly Hills, CA: Sage.

Katz, E., and Paul Lazarsfeld. 1955. *Personal Influence: The Part Played by People in the Flow of Mass Communications*. New York: Free Press.

Katz, Eliho. 1987. "Communications Research since Lazarfeld." *Public Opinion Quarterly* 51: S25–S45.

Key, V. O. 1955. "A Theory of Critical Elections." *Journal of Politics* 17: 3–18.

Klapper, Joseph. 1960. *The Effects of Mass Communications*. Glencoe, IL: Free Press.

Kornacki, Steve. 2011. "Is Olbermann the Victim of His Own Success?" *Salon.com*, Jan. 23. Available at http://www.salon.com/2011/01/22/countdown_rip. Last accessed April 24, 2013.

Krugman, Paul. 2011. "The Years of Shame." *New York Times*, Sept. 11. Available at http://krugman.blogs.nytimes.com/2011/09/11/the-years-of-shame. Last accessed July 3, 2012.

Lacy, Stephen. 1992. "The Financial Commitment Approach to News Media Competition." *Journal of Media Economics* 5: 5–21.

Ladd, Everett Carll. 1980. "Polling and the Press: The Clash of Institutional Imperatives." *Public Opinion Quarterly* 44: 574–84.

Ladd, Jonathan M. 2012. *Why Americans Hate the Media and How It Matters*. Princeton, NJ: Princeton University Press.

Lang, Kurt, and Gladys Engel Lang. 1966. "The Mass Media and Voting." In *Reader in Public Opinion and Communication*, eds. Bernard Berelson and Morris Janowitz. 2nd ed. New York: Free Press.

Larcinese, Valentino, Riccardo Puglisi, and James Snyder. 2007. "Partisan Bias in Economic News: Evidence on the Agenda Setting Behavior of US Newspapers." *NBER Working Papers*, Sept. Available at http://www.nber.org/authors_papers/valentino_larcinese. Last accessed April 23, 2013.

Lasswell, Harold. 1927. *Propaganda Technique in World War I*. Reprint Cambridge, MA: M.I.T. Press, 1971.

Lawrence, Eric, John Sides, and Henry Farrell. 2010. "Self-Segregation or Deliberation? Blog Readership, Participation, and Polarization in American Politics." *Perspectives on Politics* 8: 141–57.

Lazarsfeld, Paul, Bernard Berelson, and Hazel Gaudet. 1944. *The People's Choice*. New York: Columbia University Press.

Lee, Felicia. 2008. "Like the Candidates, TV's Political Pundits Show Signs of Diversity." *New York Times*, April 21. Last accessed June 12, 2012.

Lewis, M. 1994. "Good News, Bad News." *Psychologist* 7: 157–59.

Lichter, S. Robert, and Richard E. Noyes. 1996. *Good Intentions Make Bad News: Why Americans Hate Campaign Journalism*. Lanham, MD: Rowman & Littlefield.

Lichter, S. Robert, Stanley Rothman, and Linda Lichter. 1986. *The Media Elite: America's New Power-Brokers*. Bethesda, MD: Adler & Alder.

Lippman, Walter. 1922. *Public Opinion*. New York: Harcourt, Brace.

Loder, Kurt. 1994. "News Writing Interviews: Kurt Loder on News." *Learner.org: Teacher Professional Development*. Available at http://www.learner.org/catalog/extras/interviews/kloder/klo1.html. Last accessed May 28, 2013.

Lord, Charles G., Lee Ross, and Mark R. Lepper. 1979. "Biased Assimilation and Attitude Polarization: The Effects of Prior Theories on Subsequently Considered Evidence." *Journal of Personality and Social Psychology* 37: 2098–109.

Lott, John R. 2004. "The Impact of Early Media Election Calls on Republican Voting Rates in Florida's Western Panhandle Counties in 2000." *Public Choice* 123: 349–61.

Lynch, John. 1996. "Vanderbilt Television News Archive." Special Issue: American Film and Television Archives, *Historical Journal of Film, Radio and Television* 16(1): 81–83.

Mackuen, M. B., and S. L. Coombs. 1981. *More Than News: Media Power in Public Affairs*. Newbury Park, CA: Sage.

MacKuen, Michael, Robert S. Erikson, and James Stimson. 1989. "Macropartisanship." *American Political Science Review* 83: 1125–42.

Mak, Tim. 2012. "Gallup Poll: Conservatives Outnumber Liberals." *Politico*, Jan. 12. Available at http://www.politico.com/news/stories/0112/71385.html. Last accessed April 23, 2013.

Martin, Robert. 2001. *The Free and Open Press: The Founding of American Democratic Press Liberty*. New York: New York University Press.

Mason, Linda, Kathleen Frankovic, and Kathleen Hall Jamieson. 2001. "CBS News Coverage of Election Night 2000: Investigation, Analysis, Recommendations." Available at http://www.cbsnews.com/htdocs/c2k/pdf/REPFINAL.pdf. Last accessed April 24, 2013.

McChesney, R. 1997. *Corporate Media and the Threat to Democracy.* New York: Seven Stories.

McComas, Katherine A. 2006. "Defining Moments in Risk Communication Research: 1996–2005." *Journal of Health Communication: International Perspectives* 11: 75–91.

McCombs, Maxwell E. 2004. *Setting the Agenda: The Mass Media and Public Opinion.* Cambridge, UK: Polity.

———. 2005. "The Agenda-Setting Function of the Press." In *The Press*, eds. Geneva Overholser and Kathleen Hall Jamieson. Oxford: Oxford University Press.

McCombs, Maxwell E., and Donald L. Shaw. 1972. "The Agenda-Setting Function of Mass Media." *Public Opinion Quarterly* 36: 176–87.

McCombs, Maxwell E., and Jian-Hua Zhu. 1995. "Capacity, Diversity, and Volatility of the Public Agenda: Trends from 1954 to 1994." *Public Opinion Quarterly* 59: 495–525.

McDonald, Daniel G., and Shu-Fang Lin. 2004. "The Effect of New Networks on U.S. Television Diversity." *Journal of Media Economics* 17: 105–21.

McLeod, Jack M., Dietram A. Scheufele, and Patricia Moy. 1999. "Community, Communication, and Participation: The Role of Mass Media and Interpersonal Discussion in Local Political Participation." *Political Communication* 16: 315–36.

McManus, John. 1992. "What Kind of Commodity Is News?" *Communication Research* 19: 787–805.

———. 1994. *Market-Driven Journalism: Let the Citizen Beware.* New York: Sage.

———. 1995. "A Market-Based Model of News Production." *Communication Theory* 5: 301–38.

McQuail, Denis. 1987. *Mass Communication Theory: An Introduction.* 2nd ed. London: Sage.

Meffert, Michael F., Sungeun Chung, Amber J. Joiner, Leah Waks, and Jennifer Garst. 2006. "The Effects of Negativity and Motivated Information Processing during a Political Campaign." *Journal of Communication* 56: 27–51.

Miller, Joanne M., and Jon A. Krosnick. 2000. "News Media Impact on the Ingredients of Presidential Evaluations: Politically Knowledgeable Citizens Are Guided by a Trusted Source." *American Journal of Political Science* 44: 301–15.

Monahan, Brian. 2010. *The Shock of the News: Media Coverage and the Making of 9/11.* New York: New York University Press.

Morris, Jonathan S. 2007. "Slanted Objectivity? Perceived Media Bias, Cable News Exposure, and Political Attitudes." *Social Science Quarterly* 88: 707–28.

Mullainathen, Sendhil, and Andrei Shleifer. 2005. "The Market for News." *American Economic Review* 95: 1301–53.

Mutz, Diana C., and Byron Reeves. 2005. "The News Videomalaise: Effects of Televised Incivility on Political Trust." *American Political Science Review* 99: 1–15.

Nelson, Barbara. 1984. *Making an Issue of Child Abuse: Political Agenda Setting for Social Problems*. Chicago: University of Chicago Press.

Newhagen, John E. 1998. "TV News Images That Induce Anger, Fear, and Disgust: Effects on Approach-Avoidance and Memory." *Journal of Broadcasting & Electronic Media* 42: 265–76.

Newport, Frank. 2004. *Polling Matters: Why Leaders Must Listen to the Wisdom of the People*. New York: Warner Books.

Newton, Kenneth. 1999. "Mass Media Effects: Mobilization or Media Malaise?" *British Journal of Political Science* 29: 577–99.

Ozanich, Gary W., and Michael O. Wirth. 2004. "Structure and Change: A Communications Industry Overview." In *Media Economics: Theory and Practice*, eds. Alison Alexander, James Owers, Rod Carveth, C. Ann Hollifield, and Albert N. Greco. 3rd ed. Mahwah, NJ: Erlbaum, 71–106.

Page, Benjamin I., and Robert Y. Shapiro. 1992. *The Rational Public: Fifty Years of Trends in Americans' Policy Preferences*. Chicago: University of Chicago Press.

Patterson, Thomas E. 1994. *Out of Order*. New York: First Vintage Books.

———. 1996. "Bad News, Period." *PS: Political Science and Politics* 29: 17–20.

———. 2005. "Informing the Public." In *The Press*, eds. Geneva Overholser and Kathleen Hall Jamieson, American Institutions of Democracy. Oxford: Oxford University Press. 189–202.

Pérez-Peña, Richard. 2008. "Shrinking Ad Revenue Realigns U.S. Newspaper Industry." *New York Times*, Feb. 7.

Peterson, Iver. 1996. "Civic-Minded Pursuits Gain Ground at Newspapers." *New York Times*, March 4.

Petrocik, John. 1996. "Issue Ownership in Presidential Elections, with a 1980 Case Study." *American Journal of Political Science* 40: 825–50.

Petrocik, John, W. L. Benoit, and G. J. Hansen. 2003. "Issue Ownership and Presidential Campaigning, 1952–2000." *Political Science Quarterly* 118: 599–626.

Picard, Robert G. 2002. *The Economics and Financing of Media Companies*. New York: Fordham University Press.

———. 2005. "Money, Media, and the Public Interest." In *The Press*, eds. Geneva Overholser and Kathleen Hall Jamieson. Oxford: Oxford University Press. 337–50.

Pollock, John, and G. Dantas. 1998. "Nationwide Newspaper Coverage of Same-Sex Marriage: A Community Structure Approach." Paper presented at the Annual Meeting of the International Communication Association, Jerusalem, Israel.

Pollock, John, John Fialk, Justin Grazioli, and Kevin Sheilds. 2006. "Warrantless Wiretapping: A Community Structure Approach to Nationwide Newspaper Coverage of National Security Agency Surveillance." Paper presented at the APSA/ICA Crisis Communication Conference, Annenberg School of Communication, University of Pennsylvania, August 31, 2006.

Pollock, John, and B. Nisi. 1999. "Nationwide Newspaper Coverage of Efforts to Ban Tobacco Advertising toward Children: A Community Structure Approach." Paper presented at the Annual Meeting of International Communication Association, San Francisco, CA.

Pollock, John, C. Piccillo, D. Leopardi, S. Gratale, and K. Cabot. 2005. "Nation-wide Newspaper Coverage of Islam Post-September 11: A Community Structure Approach." *Communication Research Reports* 22: 15–27.

Pollock, John, S. Schumacher, L. de Zutter, and E. Mitchell. 2006. "Gay Rights: Nation-wide Newspaper Coverage of Gays in the Boy Scouts, Gay Adoption, and Gay Mar-riage." Paper presented at the Annual Meeting of the International Communication Association, Dresden, Germany.

Pollock, John, and S. Yulis. 2004. "Nationwide Newspaper Coverage of Physician Assisted Suicide: A Community Structure Approach." *Journal of Health Communi-cations* 9: 1–27.

Pope, Jeremy C., and Jonathan Woon. 2009. "Measuring Changes in American Party Reputations, 1939–2004." *Political Research Quarterly* 62: 653–61.

Powers, Angela. 2001. "Toward Monopolistic Competition in U.S. Local Television News." *Journal of Media Economics* 14: 77–86.

Price, Cindy. 2003. "Interfering Owners or Meddling Advertisers: How Network Tele-vision News Correspondents Feel about Ownership and Advertiser Influence on News Stories." *Journal of Media Economics* 16: 175–88.

Prior, Markus. 2005. "News vs. Entertainment: How Increasing Media Choice Widens Gaps in Political Knowledge and Turnout." *American Journal of Political Science* 49: 577–92.

Puglisi, Riccardo. 2011. "Being the *New York Times*: The Political Behaviour of a News-paper." *The B.E. Journal of Economic Analysis & Policy* 11: article 20.

Puglisi, Riccardo, and James Snyder. 2008. "Media Coverage of Political Scandals." NBER Working Paper No. 14598. December. Available at http://www.nber.org/papers/w14598.pdf. Last accessed April 24, 2013.

———. 2011. "Newspaper Coverage of Political Scandals." *Journal of Politics* 73(3): 1–20.

Putnam, Robert D. 1995. "Tuning in, Tuning Out: The Strange Disappearance of Social Capital in America." *PS: Political Science and Politics* 28: 664–83.

Robinson, Michael J. 1976. "Public Affairs Television and the Growth of Political Malaise: The Case of 'the Selling of the Pentagon.'" *American Political Science Review* 70: 409–32.

Rogers, Everett M., and James W. Dearing. 2007. "Agenda-Setting Research: Where Has It Been, Where Is It Going?" In *Media Power in Politics*, ed. Doris Graber. 5th ed. Washington, DC: CQ Press.

Rogers, Everett M., James W. Dearing, and S. Chang. 1991. "AIDS in the 1980s: The Agenda-Setting Process of a Public Issue." *Journalism Monographs* 126 (April).

Romer, Daniel, Kathleen Hall Jamieson, and Sean Aday. 2003. "Television News and the Cultivation of Fear of Crime." *Journal of Communication* 53(1): 88–104.

Romer, Daniel, Kathleen Hall Jamieson, and Josh Pasek. 2009. "Building Social Capital in Young People: The Role of Mass Media and Life Outlook." *Political Communica-tion* 26: 65–83.

Rosenstiel, Tom. 2005. "Political Polling and the New Media Culture: A Case of More Being Less." *Public Opinion Quarterly* 69: 698–715.

Rosenstiel, Tom, Marion Just, Todd Belt, Atiba Pertilla, Walter Dean, and Dante Chinni. 2007. *We Interrupt This Broadcast: How to Improve Local News and Win Ratings, Too.* Boston: Cambridge University Press.

Russo, Frank D. 1971–1972. "A Study of Bias in TV Coverage of the Vietnam War: 1969 and 1970." *Public Opinion Quarterly* 35: 539–43.

Sabato, Larry J., Mark Stencel, and S. Robert Lichter. 2000. *Peepshow: Media and Politics in an Age of Scandal.* Lanham, MD: Rowman & Littlefield.

Sanford, Bruce W., and Jane E. Kirtley. 2005. "The First Amendment Tradition and Its Critics." In *The Press,* eds. Geneva Overholser and Kathleen Hall Jamieson. Oxford: Oxford University Press. 263–76.

Schneider, Saundra K., and William G. Jacoby. 2005. "Elite Discourse and American Public Opinion: The Case of Welfare Spending." *Political Research Quarterly* 58: 367–79.

Schudson, Michael. 1998. *The Good Citizen: A History of American Civic Life.* New York: Martin Kessler.

Selepak, Andrew G. 2006. "New Evidence of Liberal Media Bias." *Accuracy in Media,* Nov. 6. Available at http://www.aim.org/aim-report/aim-report-new-evidence-of-liberal-media-bias-november-a. Last accessed April 24, 2013.

Shaw, Donald R., and Bartholomew H. Sparrow. 1999. "From the Inner Ring Out: News Congruence, Cue-Taking, and Campaign Coverage." *Political Research Quarterly* 52: 323–51.

Shaw, E. 1977. "The Interpersonal Agenda." In *The Emergence of American Public Issues: The Agenda-Setting Function of the Press,* eds. D. Shaw and Maxwell E. McCombs. St. Paul, MN: West.

Sheilds, Todd G., Robert K. Goidel, and Barry Tadlock. 1995. "The Net Impact of Media Exposure on Individual Voting Decisions in U.S. Senate and House Elections." *Legislative Studies Quarterly* 20: 415–30.

Shelter, Brian. 2010. "With Tagline, MSNBC Embraces a Political Identity." *New York Times,* Oct. 4. Available at http://www.nytimes.com/2010/10/05/business/media/05adco.html?_r=2. Last accessed April 24, 2013.

Sherman, Gabriel. 2010. "Chasing Fox." *New York Magazine,* Oct. 3. Available at http://nymag.com/news/media/68717. Last accessed April 24, 2013.

Shoemaker, P. J. 1996. "Hardwired for News: Using Biological and Cultural Evolution to Explain the Surveillance Function." *Journal of Communication* 36: 32–47.

Sides, John. 2006. "The Origin of Campaign Agendas." *British Journal of Political Science* 36: 407–36.

Simon, J. L. 1980. "Resources, Population, Environment: An Oversupply of False Bad News." *Science* 208: 1431–37.

Sims, Christopher A. 1980. "Macroeconomics and Reality." *Econometrica* 48: 1–48.

Slattery, Karen, Mark Doremus, and Linda Marcus. 2001. "Shifts in Public Affairs Reporting on the Network Evening News: A Move toward the Sensational." *Journal of Broadcasting & Electronic Media* 45: 290–302.

Smith, Adam. 1904. *An Inquiry into the Nature and Causes of the Wealth of Nations.* Edited by Edwin Cannan. 5th ed. London: Methuen.

Smith, B. L., Harold Lasswell, and R. D. Casey. 1946. *Propaganda, Communication, and Public Opinion: A Comprehensive Reference Guide.* Princeton, NJ: Princeton University Press.

Smith, Kim 1987a. "Newspaper Coverage and Public Concern about Community Issues: A Time-Series Analysis." In *Journalism Monographs* 101. Columbia, SC: Association for Education in Journalism and Mass Communication.

———. 1987b. "Effects of Newspaper Coverage on Community Issue Concerns and Local Government." *Communication Research* 14: 379–95.

Smith, Tom W. 1980. "America's Most Important Problem: A Trend Analysis, 1946–1976." *Public Opinion Quarterly* 44: 164–80.

Sotirovic, Mira, and Jack M. McLeod. 2001. "Values, Communication Behavior, and Political Participation." *Political Communication* 18: 273–300.

Stevenson, R., William J. Gonzenbach, and D. Prabu. 1994. "Economic Recession and the News." *Mass Communication Review* 21: 4–19.

Sutter, Daniel. 2001. "Can the Media Be So Liberal? The Economics of Media Bias." *Cato Journal* 20: 431–51.

Tan, Alexis S. 1980. "Mass Media Use, Issue Knowledge, and Political Involvement." *Public Opinion Quarterly* 44: 241–48.

Tewksbury, David, and Jason Rittenberg. 2012. *News on the Internet: Information and Citizenship in the 21st Century.* New York: Oxford University Press.

Tichenor, P. J., G. A. Donohue, and C. N. Olien. 1970. "Mass Media Flow and Differential Growth in Knowledge." *Public Opinion Quarterly* 34: 159–70.

Trumbo, Craig Warren. 1995. "Longitudinal Modeling of Public Issues: An Application of the Agenda-Setting Process to the Issue of Global Warming." *Journalism and Communication Monographs* 152.

Tuchman, Gaye. 1978. *Making News: A Study in the Construction of Reality.* New York: Free Press.

Turner, Joel. 2007. "The Messenger Overwhelming the Message: Ideological Cues and Perceptions of Bias in Television News." *Political Behavior* 29: 441–64.

Turrow, Joseph. 1983. "Local Television: Producing Soft News." *Journal of Communication* 33(2): 111–23.

Underwood, Doug. 1993. *When MBAs Rule the Newsroom.* New York: Columbia University Press.

Valentino, Nicholas A., Matthew N. Beckmann, and Thomas A. Buhr. 2001. "A Spiral of Cynicism for Some: The Contingent Effects of Campaign News Frames on Participation and Confidence in Government." *Political Communication* 18: 347–67.

Van Hoffman, Nicholas. 1980. "Public Opinion Polls: Newspapers Making Their Own News?" *Public Opinion Quarterly* 44: 572–73.

Vincent, Richard C., and Michael D. Basil. 1997. "College Students' News Gratifications, Media Use, and Current Events Knowledge." *Journal of Broadcasting & Electronic Media* 41: 380–92.

Wade, Serena, and Wilbur Schramm. 1969. "The Mass Media as Sources of Public Affairs, Science, and Health Knowledge." *Public Opinion Quarterly* 33: 197–209.

Walgrave, Stefaan, Jonas Lefevere, and Michiel Nuytemans. 2009. "Issue Ownership Stability and Change: How Political Parties Claim and Maintain Issues through Media Appearances." *Political Communication* 26: 153–72.

Walgrave, Stefaan, and Peter Van Aelst. 2006. "The Contingency of the Mass Media's Political Agenda Setting Power: Toward a Preliminary Theory." *Journal of Communication* 56: 88–109.

Wanta, Wayne, Mary Ann Stephenson, Judy Vanslyke Turk, and Maxwell E. McCombs. 1989. "How the President's State of the Union Talk Influenced News Media Agendas." *Journalism Quarterly* 66: 537–41.

Weaver, David H. 1996. "What Voters Learn from Media." *Annals of the American Academy of Political and Social Science* 546: 34–47.

———. 2005. "Journalists' Views on Public Opinion and Civic Journalism." Paper presented at the Annual Meeting of the International Communication Association, New York, NY.

Whitman, David. 1996. "The Myth of AWOL Parents." *U.S. News & World Report*, July 1, 54–56.

Whitson, Jennifer A., and Adam D. Galinsky. 2008. "Lacking Control Increases Illusory Pattern Perception." *Science* 322: 115–17.

Winship, Elizabeth C., and W. Allport Gordon. 1943. "Do Rosy Headlines Sell Newspapers?" *Public Opinion Quarterly* 7: 205–10.

Yousef, Miranda. "Diversity on Our Air: 'Black in America 2' Comes to CNN." *International Documentary Association.* 2009. Available at http://www.documentary.org/content/diversity-our-air-black-america-2-comes-cnn. Last accessed June 10, 2013.

Zaller, John. 1991. "Information, Values, and Opinion." *American Political Science Review* 85: 1215–37.

———. 1998. "The Rule of Product Substitution in Presidential Campaign News." *Annals of the American Academy of Political and Social Science* 560: 111–28.

Community Development and Housing, as issue area, 59–64, 67, 69
Condit, Gary, 99
Congress: appearance, 8; corruption, 25; funding journalism, 145, 153; legislation, 23, 34, 82, 100
constitutional protection, 10–11, 40, 55–56
content analysis, 58, 95
Cooper, Anderson, 120, 131, 134
C-SPAN, 156

Darwin, Charles, 8
Defense as issue area, 54, 59–64, 67, 68, 99–100, 104; as Republican issue, 95, 97, 101, 106, 142
demand-side model, 5–6, 26, 32–39
Dobbs, Lou, 83, 92
Donahue, Phil, 87, 113, 137

echo chamber, 76. See also ideological bias
economic incentives: for firms, 3–4, 12, 26, 40, 45, 77, 112; effects of, on democracy, 14
education, as issue area, 59–64, 67, 69
Edwards, John, 125
Energy as issue area, 59–60, 62–64, 67–68
evolutionary psychology, 21

Federal Communications Commission, 82, 152
Federal Government Operations, as issue area, 59–64, 67
Florida: 2000 recount, 86; 2011 Casey Anthony murder trial, 104; 2012 Trayvon Martin shooting, 117, 124
Food and Drug Administration, 10
Fox News Channel, 84–92; anchors, 36; as cable news outlet, 105; conservative bias, 32, 37, 73–74, 93, 116–119, 129, 131–133, 139, 146, 150 ; contributors, 127–128; *Hannity*, 158; *The O'Reilly Factor*, 73, 113, 116–117, 121, 123–126, 128–129, 154, 158; *Special Report*, 116–117, 121
Friedman, Milton, 137–138
Friendly, Fred, 110

Gallup's Most Important Problem question (MIP), 64–65, 98

"game-schema" coverage, 16. See also campaign
Gergen, David, 131, 134
Gingrich, Newt, 117
Giuliani, Rudy, 122
Granger analysis, 66–67, 69, 101
Griffin, Phil, 89–90

Hannity, Sean, 85
hard news, 16, 111; CNN, 84; FNC, 116. See also traditional journalism
Health as issue area, 59–60, 62–64, 67, 69
Headline News (HLN) network, 84, 91
horse-race coverage, 16, 35, 156. See also campaign
Huffington Post, 89
hypodermic needle theory, 46. See also propaganda

ideological bias: in analysis, 57; Conservative, 32, 85; Liberal, 30–31, 32, 82–83, 85; in the market, 37–40, 55, 138–139, 144, 160
ideological median, 83
ideology: in cable news, 82–93, 104, 107, 142, 146; political, 39, 47, 75, 77–81, 114, 116, 142, 146, 159
incentive structure, 8–10, 109
Ingraham, Laura, 85
Inside Edition, 73
International Affairs, as issue area, 59–65, 67
"invisible hand," 8, 10
Iran-Contra, 61
issue: agenda, 22, 44, 63, 142; area, 58, 59, 74, 94, 96–97, 100; convergence, 58; coverage, 75, 81, 93, 98, 103–104; party-owned, 95–100, 102–106, 142; salience, 22, 48, 53, 57–58, 65–67, 70, 74

Kelly, Megan, 36, 125
Kerry, John, 30
Key Journalistic Standards, 27
Keyes, Alan, 88, 113
Koppel, Ted, 1–2, 4, 13, 77, 137–138
Krauthammer, Charles, 86, 127–130
Krugman, Paul, 122, 158

ABOUT THE AUTHOR

Joseph E. Uscinski teaches and researches in American Politics. He earned his PhD at the University of Arizona and is currently Assistant Professor of Political Science at the University of Miami.

CPSIA information can be obtained
at www.ICGtesting.com
Printed in the USA
FFOW02n1002220816
27018FF